Inland Fishes
of
Rhode Island
by
Alan D. Libby

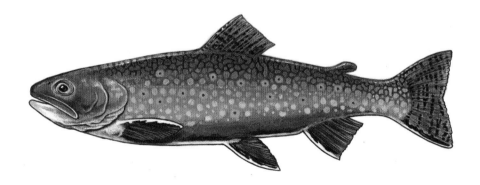

Illustrations by

Robert Jon Golder

Rhode Island
Division of Fish and Wildlife
Department of Environmental Management

West Kingston, Rhode Island

ISBN 978-0-9834581-0-4 (hardcover)

ISBN 978-0-9834581-1-1 (paperback)

Library of Congress Control Number: 2012939230

Published with funding from the U. S. Fish and Wildlife Service, Wildlife and Sportfish Restoration Program.

This program receives Federal funds from the U. S. Fish and Wildlife Service. Regulations of the U. S. Department of the Interior strictly prohibit unlawful discrimination in departmental Federally Assisted Programs on the basis of race, color, national origin or ancestry, gender, sexual orientation, age, or disability. Any person who believes he or she has been discriminated against in this program, activity, or facility operated by this recipient of Federal assistance should write to: The Office for Equal Opportunity, U. S. Department of the Interior, Office of the Secretary, Washington, D. C. 20240.

Contents

Figures

Tables

Acknowledgements

I am indebted to the many summer interns who assisted me over the years with hundreds of field surveys, as this publication would not have been possible without their assistance. My thanks are extended to my colleagues Charlie Brown, Michelle Burnett, Dave Dumuchellle, Christine Dudley, Phil Edwards, Dennis Erkan, Jeff Estes, Tom Evans, Ted Gartland, John Giramma, Todd Greene, Tom Griffith, Pat Houlihan, Ray Jobin, Bill Lapin, Christine Lipsky, John MacCoy, John O'Brien, Scott Olszewski, Houston Ponte, Chris Powell, Dennis Ryan, Dick Satchwill, Eric Schneider, and Kim Sullivan who also assisted me in a variety of ways. I also thank William Krueger, Jim Lake, Steve Ryba, and John Serbst for their assistance and to the private landowners, municipalities, water departments, and water districts that provided access to the many water bodies where there was no public access. I especially thank Veronica Masson who, in addition to assisting with collections and reviewing the original document, designed and edited this publication and Chris Raithel for his critical review and advice. And finally, I thank Robert Golder for his fine art work and advice. This project was funded by the RI Division of Fish & Wildlife through the U.S. Fish and Wildlife Service, Sport Fish Restoration Project RI-F-20-R.

In memory of
my wife Moira.

Introduction

Fish are widely distributed in the aquatic environment. Their distribution is influenced within this environment by numerous natural and anthropogenic or manmade factors.

Natural Factors

Freshwaters can be grouped according to whether the water is flowing (lotic) or whether it is standing (lentic). The distribution of fish in these environments is predictable, for the most part. Species such as the blacknose dace and fallfish are more likely to occur in lotic environments, whereas species such as the golden shiner and largemouth bass prefer lentic environments. The distribution of fish in the lotic environment may be influenced further by the velocity of the water. Species, including the Atlantic salmon and longnose dace, are generally found in the more rapidly flowing reaches of streams, whereas the common shiner and fallfish are more likely to be found in moderately flowing areas.

Elevation and gradient are topographical features that appear in the physiography or geomorphology of the earth's surface. They not only influence weather patterns and air temperatures, but also water velocities. The Northeast contains a variety of physiographic regions that include mountainous areas where elevations range from the 6,288 foot summit of Mount Washington, New Hampshire, to sea level areas along the Atlantic Coast. Within these physiographic regions are a great variety of habitats. Unlike other states in the Northeast,

Figure 1. Rocky substrates and undercut banks provide hiding places for brook trout, Atlantic salmon (stocked), blacknose dace, and redfin pickerel in Parris Brook.

Rhode Island contains just two physiographic regions, the New England Uplands Section and the Seaboard Lowlands Section (Fenneman 1938) and thus a fewer number of habitats. The New England Uplands Section, located for the most part in the western part of the state, is characterized by rolling hills with moderately flowing streams. The highest point in Rhode Island, the 812 foot Jerimoth Hill, is found in this region. The Coastal Lowlands Section is a region where elevations are lower and the topography is generally less hilly. Streams in this region are generally warmer and tend to flow more slowly.

Cover is an important physical feature that affects the distribution of fish. Cover, in the form of aquatic vegetation, undercut river banks, woody debris, overhanging brush, or rocky substrates provide places where fish can rest or hide (Figure 1). Open areas with little or no cover tend to contain fewer, if any fish.

Salinity is an important chemical factor affecting fish distribution. Estuaries, semi-enclosed bodies of water that are located in coastal areas, have salinities that vary widely. Because of the wide variation in salinities, ranging from zero to more than 30 parts per thousand, estuaries (Figure 2) often support a large diversity of fishes, including marine and freshwater species compared to areas where the waters are entirely fresh (Figure 3). Since young fish often have different physical and chemical requirements than mature fish, the young of many marine species such as the Atlantic menhaden, crevalle jack, and weakfish may temporarily utilize estuaries as nursery areas during the late summer and fall before moving into the marine environment. Species that generally remain in the estuarine environment throughout the year include the striped killifish and rainwater killifish. Freshwater species such as the largemouth bass and chain pickerel often stray into the upper reaches of an estuary.

Figure 2. Pawcatuck River Estuary, Westerly. More than 40 species of freshwater, diadromous, and marine fish were collected in this area which is located below the head-of-tide. Species include: chain pickerel, largemouth bass, redbreast sunfish, alewife, American shad, striped bass, Atlantic menhaden, Atlantic needlefish, crevalle jack, and winter flounder.

Temperature and oxygen concentrations also affect fish distributions. Species like the brook trout prefer the cooler, well-oxygenated waters of headwater streams, whereas species such as the fallfish favor the warmer and slower-flowing reaches of streams. Oxygen concentrations are affected by water temperature. For example, an increase in temperature reduces the amount of oxygen in the water and in turn affects the overall distribution of fish in a stream or pond. Temperature not only affects the distribution of fish in a watershed or drainage basin but it also influences, among other things, the timing of fish migrations, the initiation of spawning, incubation time of eggs, and growth rates.

The last ice age may have played a role in the distribution of freshwater fish in Rhode Island. During the Wisconsinan Ice Age, freshwater fish were displaced by a large ice sheet that once covered much of North America. Long Island, Block Island, and the islands of Martha's Vineyard and Nantucket are the obvious remnants of a terminal moraine that was formed during this period (Raymo and Raymo 1989). Then approximately 17,000 years ago, as temperatures moderated, the glacier began to recede. The receding glacier allowed fish that were located in refugia to recolonize post-glaciated areas. The distribution of fish among the various drainages in New England and the routes they may have utilized has been postulated (Schmidt 1986; Whitworth 1996).

In summary, fish occupy a wide variety of habitats by being both physiologically and behaviorally adapted to the environment. Combinations of certain physical and chemical properties can further influence their distribution. Their ultimate distributions are determined by a combination of these factors.

Anthropogenic Factors

Human intervention has played a large role in altering the

Figure 3. Upper Pawcatuck River, Charlestown/ Richmond. Thirteen species, American eel, bluegill, black crappie, brown bullhead, chain pickerel, fallfish, largemouth bass, pumpkinseed, redfin pickerel, white catfish, white perch, white sucker, and yellow perch were collected in this segment of the river, which is located well above the head-of-tide.

distribution of fish in Rhode Island. Beginning in the 1790s with the industrial revolution, dams were built on many of the state's rivers and streams to impound water to power mills. Dams created insurmountable barriers to such species as the American shad and Atlantic salmon that were returning to natal rivers to spawn. Dam construction eventually led to the extirpation of the Atlantic salmon in Rhode Island.

Connectivity has been restored to parts of some rivers with the construction of fishways (Figures 4 & 5). The first fishway in Rhode Island was reported by the Commissioners of Inland Fisheries (CIF) as being built at the mouth of the Pawtuxet River in 1873 (CIF 1874). Dams not only block upstream migrations and fragment habitats but they also have negative impacts on the distribution of fish in both upstream and downstream areas (Winston and Taylor 1991; Kanehl et al. 1997; Guenther and Spacie

Figure 4. An Alaskan steep pass fish ladder at the Gilbert Stuart Birthplace.

2006).

Impoundments, created by more than 600 dams (OCI 2004), have also affected rivers and streams by converting free-flowing waters into lentic environments and by altering the water's thermal characteristics. Water temperatures increase when streams that were once entirely shaded by the forest canopy are now impounded and fully exposed to the warming effects of the sun. Consequently, fish requiring cool flowing waters of streams (Figure 6) are forced to move to areas that are more suitable and, in turn, are replaced by lentic species that prefer the warmer standing waters of impoundments (Figure 7).

Another example of human intervention has been the introduction of nonnative fish species. These introductions began in Rhode Island in 1870 with the stocking of smallmouth bass (CIF 1872). Since 1870 more than ten nonnative species have become naturalized in the state's freshwaters. Native species, such as brook trout and white perch, were also widely stocked throughout the state. The purpose of the introductions was to provide more sport and food fish for anglers, because it was realized that the supply of native fish in streams and ponds was not inexhaustible (CIF 1911). The illegal release of such species as the goldfish (*Carassius auratus*) and banded cichlid (*Chichlasoma severum*) by both aquarists and anglers has contributed to the placement of unwanted nonnative species in local waters. The geographical range of many species has been altered to such a degree that their original distribution is questionable.

Figure 5. A Denil fish ladder, with juvenile low slot board diverter, at the Forge Road dam on the Potowomut (Hunt) River.

The demand for freshwater for irrigation and drinking water also threatens aquatic habitat and affects the distribution of fish. Water withdrawals from aquifers and streams alter stream flows and instream habitat, forcing fish and other organisms to move to downstream areas. Water withdrawals also reduce the diversity and abundance of fish, degrade spawning and nursery habitats, disrupt fish passage, and decrease protective cover, which ultimately increases the susceptibility of fish to predation. Those fish and invertebrates trapped in pools left by receding water are not only exposed to increased predation, but also to higher water temperatures, lower dissolved oxygen concentrations and ultimately death if the pool completely dries. The desiccation of exposed substrate also means there is a loss of benthic organisms for fish to feed upon when water levels return to normal. The demand for water is particularly crucial during the summer months when flows are naturally low and becomes even more exacerbated during droughts. There have been cases of river and stream segments completely drying up as a result of withdrawals. Effective resource management is imperative for maintaining ecological integrity.

Previous Studies

The study of the fishes of Rhode Island began in 1898 when the CIF authorized a "Systematic examination of the physical and biological conditions of Narragansett Bay" (CIF 1899). Based on fish that were collected in fish traps, washed ashore, or were caught by angling, the first list of fishes of Narragansett Bay was formulated in 1899 (CIF 1900). This list, which also contained many freshwater species, was expanded in 1905 to include such information as geographical distribution, habitat, and season (Tracy 1906). The list was again revised and published in a report entitled "Annotated List of Fishes Known to Inhabit the Waters of Rhode Island" (Tracy 1910), which contains additional information on geographical distribution, habitat, and reproduction. A more recent list of the freshwater fishes of Rhode Island was formulated (Krueger 2001).

Figure 6. Breakheart Brook, Exeter, is a coldwater stream dominated by brook trout, but also contains fallfish, tessellated darter, white sucker, American eel, and stocked Atlantic salmon.

The need for a systematic survey of streams and ponds became apparent when many of the fish that were being stocked did not survive. In 1939 a survey was initiated, by what was then called the Division of Fish & Game, to collect physical, chemical, and biological data on streams to determine their suitability for stocking (DA&C 1939, 1940; Fellows 1940). Streams located on state property were also examined in terms of their suitability for stream improvement. To determine the status of fish populations in lakes and ponds, a survey was initiated in 1952 to collect physical, chemical, and biological data (DA&C 1953). The first phase of this survey culminated in a report on 41 lakes and ponds by Saila and Horton (1957). The lake and pond survey continued with the survey of 60 more lakes and ponds, bringing the total number surveyed to 101 (Guthrie and Stolgitis 1977). From 1962 to 1966, 39 streams and 17 ponds were surveyed in the Pawcatuck River watershed (Guthrie et al. 1973). Between 1973 and 1979, streams in the Blackstone (Demaine and Guthrie 1979), Saugatucket (Demaine and O'Brien 1980), Moosup (Guthrie 1980), and Hunt (Demaine 1981) River watersheds were also surveyed. Fisheries investigations were also conducted in two Block Island ponds, Fresh and Sachem Ponds, in 1987 to augment water quality investigations (Lapin and Libby 1987).

Each year the Division of Fish and Wildlife receives numerous requests from a variety of sources including government agencies seeking fish population data for research or for permit applications, university researchers, or from the general public seeking information on fish populations in selected streams and ponds. In order to respond to these requests, and to protect and manage the freshwater fishery resources of the state, current information was required. Consequently, in 1993 a comprehensive statewide survey was initiated to collect physical, chemical, and fishery data on streams and ponds located in each of the state's watersheds. This publication is the culmination of that effort. It provides information on the distribution and relative abundance of each species collected, a summary, by species, of the physical and chemical parameters encountered during the survey, and it aids the reader in identifying species of fish that were observed.

Figure 7. Breakheart Pond, West Greenwich and Exeter, is a 48 acre impoundment on Breakheart Brook, that was dominated by ten warmwater species: American eel, bluegill, banded sunfish, chain pickerel, creek chubsucker, golden shiner, large-mouth bass, pumpkinseed, white sucker, and yellow perch.

Methods
Study Area

The watersheds of Rhode Island were divided into ten drainage basins, the Blackstone, Thames, Pawtuxet, Pawcatuck, Woonasquatucket, Moshassuck, Hunt, and Saugatucket River basins, and into the coastal drainages of Narragansett Bay and the Atlantic Ocean (Figure 8). The Pawtuxet, Woonasquatucket, Saugatucket, Moshassuck, and Hunt River drainage basins lie entirely within the state's borders.

Portions of the remaining basins lie within the neighboring states of Connecticut or Massachusetts. The Blackstone River basin, located for the most part in Massachusetts, encompasses an area of approximately 454 mi^2. Approximately 120 mi^2 (25%) of this basin lies within northern Rhode Island. The Thames River basin, totaling more than 1200 mi^2 lies primarily within the eastern portion of Connecticut and southern-central Massachusetts. A small portion of the Thames River basin, 61 mi^2 (5%), lies in the extreme western part of the state. The Pawtuxet drainage basin, situated primarily in the middle of the state, drains an area of approximately 235 mi^2. The Pawcatuck River basin drains an area of approximately 320 mi^2. A major portion of the Pawcatuck basin, approximately 250 mi^2 (80%), lies within the southwestern part of Rhode Island. The remaining portion of the Pawcatuck basin is located in eastern Connecticut. The Woonasquatucket and Moshassuck River drainages, sandwiched between the Pawtuxet and Blackstone River basins, drain areas of approximately 50 mi^2 and 25 mi^2, respectively. The Hunt and Saugatucket River drainages, found between the Pawcatuck and Narragansett Bay drainage basins, drain areas of approximately 25 mi^2 and 30 mi^2, respectively.

The two remaining drainages, the Narragansett Bay and Atlantic Ocean, consist, for the most part, of a collection of small coastal streams and ponds that occur along the shores of the state. Several relatively large drainages that are located primarily in the state of Massachusetts, the Ten Mile, Runnins, and Taunton River drainages, were included in the Narragansett Bay drainage as only a small portion of them actually flows through Rhode Island. Similarly, Adamsville Brook, a tributary of the Westport River of Massachusetts, was included in the Atlantic Ocean drainage.

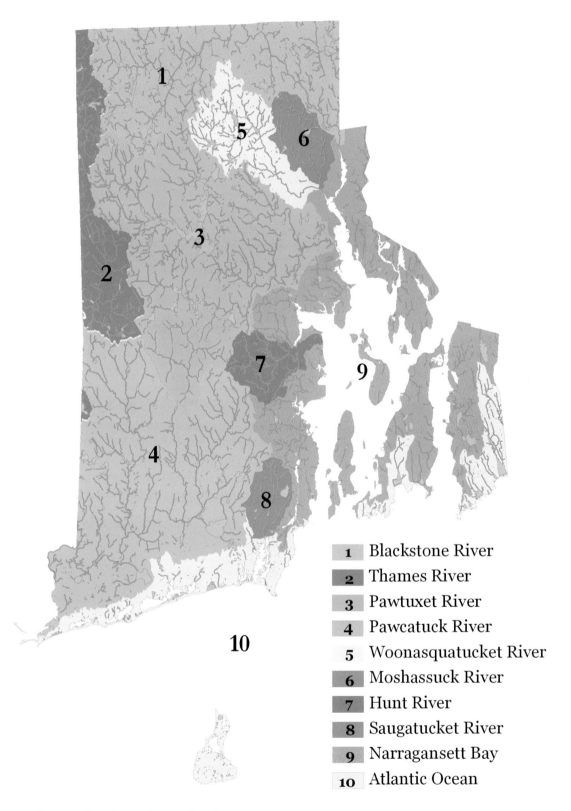

1   Blackstone River
2   Thames River
3   Pawtuxet River
4   Pawcatuck River
5   Woonasquatucket River
6   Moshassuck River
7   Hunt River
8   Saugatucket River
9   Narragansett Bay
10   Atlantic Ocean

Figure 8. Rhode Island Drainage basins.

Field sampling

Fish were collected primarily by electrofishing (Figures 9 & 10). In selected ponds and the mainstems of large nonwadeable rivers with suitable access, electrofishing was generally conducted at night during the spring with a Smith-Root Model SR-16 electrofishing boat that was equipped with a 5.0-GPP generator and a pair of one-meter umbrella anode arrays, each equipped with six stainless steel droppers (Figure 9). The cathode is insulated from the hull and mounted across the bow. In

Figure 9. The electrofishing boat.

ponds smaller than 50 acres (20 ha), electrofishing was conducted along the entire length of the shoreline (Table 1). The shorelines of lakes larger than 50 acres were divided into 12 sampling areas. Sampling was conducted at a single location that was randomly selected within each sampling area in an attempt to sample all the major littoral habitat types. An exception to this procedure was the Flat River Reservoir (a.k.a. Johnson Pond). Because of the long, convoluted nature of the shoreline [28 miles (44.7 km) of shoreline vs. 659 acres (267 ha) of surface area], the Flat River Reservoir was divided into 24 sampling areas and sampled over a two-night period.

Wadeable streams were sampled with a Smith-Root Model 12-A or Coffelt Model BP-4 backpack electrofishing unit during the daytime from June to September, when flows are normally low (Figure 10). Sampling during periods of abnormally high flows,

Figure 10. Backpack electrofishing in a wadeable stream.

Figure 11. Beach seining.

(e.g., immediately following heavy rains) was avoided. The electrofishing crew generally consisted of an operator and two netters. Stream stations that were extremely wide were sampled simultaneously with two backpack electrofishing crews. An attempt was made to select stations that contained a variety of habitats such as pools, runs, and riffles. A single pass was carefully conducted in the streambed, in an upstream direction, which included all types of microhabitats such as beds of aquatic macrophytes, woody debris, and undercut banks when present. In an attempt to maximize the number of fish species collected at a station, the length of stream surveyed was at least 35 times its mean width (Lyons 1992). This was not always possible because of the shallow nature of several streams caused by extreme drought, dense shoreline vegetation, and/or soft bottom sediments. Block nets were not used.

The selection of sampling stations was based on accessibility. Ponds and the mainstems of large rivers had to be easily accessible by boat. Stream stations had to be wadeable, usually less than one meter in depth, and located in close proximity to a road. Any pond or stream with suitable access was selected.

To augment the stream and pond survey, supplementary fish sampling was conducted in ponds that had been previously sampled with the electrofishing boat in an attempt to collect any species that may have escaped capture during the original survey. Supplementary sampling was also conducted at several locations, both stream and pond locations, where electrofishing was

Figure 12. A fyke or trap net in the Big River.

unsuitable because of high salinities (e.g., lower Pawcatuck River, lower Jamestown Brook, Prince Pond Stream, and Wesquage Pond) or where there was no suitable access for the electrofishing boat (e.g., Killingly Pond). The sole purpose of supplementary sampling was to identify the presence of individual species of fish. Several techniques, that included seines, gill nets, trap nets, and diving, were utilized (Figure 11 & 12).

Data

All fish were identified and enumerated. Almost all of the fish collected were identified in the field and released alive except for small, difficult specimens, which were preserved in formalin and identified later in the laboratory. Excluding fish collected during supplementary sampling, total lengths were measured for at least 30 individuals of a species.

The following data were also recorded at each location: sampling duration; station length, width, and depth (stream only); land use and percent canopy (visual estimates of the canopy were expressed as a proportion of the stream station that was shaded); temperature (air and water); dissolved oxygen concentration; pH; conductivity; bottom type (visual estimates of each substrate type, listed below); and the presence or absence of aquatic vegetation and woody debris.

A list of Substrate types used in the stream assessments

Substrate Types	Size/Description
Bedrock	
Boulder	>254 mm (>10 inches)
Cobble	64-254 mm (2.5-10 inches)
Gravel	2-64 mm (0.1-2.5 inches)
Sand	0.06-2 mm
Silt	0.004-0.06 mm
Muck-mud	Soft, silty, black organic material
Detritus	Coarse plant material, sticks, leaves
Marl	A mixture of carbonates and shell material

Physical and chemical parameters encountered during the survey are summarized by fish species and pond. The distribution and relative abundance of fish are also summarized. Locations where an individual fish species was collected were plotted on maps developed from the Rhode Island Geographical Information System (RIGIS). RIGIS is the property of the Rhode Island Board of Governors for Higher Education.

Table 1. - Physical and chemical characteristics of the ponds that were sampled during the 1993-2007 Stream & Pond Survey. Substrate abbreviations are as follows: Bd = bedrock, B = boulder, C = Cobble, G = gravel, S = sand, Sl = silt, M = muck/mud, and D = detritus.

Water Body/ Station	Area (ha)	Max. depth (m)	Mean depth (m)	Basin	Shoreline (km)	Substrate	Conductivity (µS)	pH	DO (mg/l)	Water Temp. (°C)
Alton Pond/4.2.31	16	1.8	1.2	Manmade	2.8	Unknown	96	7.70	10.05	15.2
Asa Pond/8.0.3	11	1.2	1.1	Manmade	1.4	Unknown	128	6.41	9.31	16.1
Ashville Pond/4.2.7	10	3.7	1.2	Manmade	1.7	D,B,C	33	4.85	8.40	20
Barber Pond/4.4.2	11	5.8	3.4	Natural	1.8	D,G,S,Sl	64	6.25	8.40	21
Beach Pond/2.2.4	170	19.8	9.1	Manmade	8.8	G	72	5.50	8.90	18.5
Belleville Pond/9.a.1	64	2.4	1.5	Manmade	4.4	Unknown	150	6.70	9.65	18.2
Blue Pond/4.2.10	37	7.6	2.4	Manmade	3.4	M,G,B,C,S	32	4.91	9.21	25.5
Boone Lake/4.2.4	19	5.5	3.7	Manmade	2.6	B,G,S,C,D	233	6.71	9.28	18.5
Bowdish Reservoir/2.2.3	92	3.4	1.7	Manmade	5.4	Sl	72	5.50	8.60	18.5
Breakheart Pond/4.2.5	18	2.1	1.2	Manmade	2	D,M	74	6.14	8.65	20.2
Brickyard Pond/9.b.22	41	5.5	3.4	Manmade	1.5	Unknown	3440	7.80	10.27	18.4
Browning Mill Pond/4.2.6	19	1.8	1.2	Manmade	2	D,M,B,G	206	6.78	8.68	21
Burlingame Reservoir/1.4.12	28	2.4	0.9	Manmade	3.4	Unknown	38	4.45	10.97	15.5
Carbuncle Pond/2.1.4	14	7.3	4.6	Natural	1.8	G,S,Sl,D	54	6.70	8.70	21.5
Carr Pond/3.3.7	32	10.7	4.3	Manmade	2.4	G,S	38	5.12	9.00	21.3
Central Pond/9.b.21	53	-	1.5	Manmade	7.7	Unknown	387	7.54	11.47	17.5
Chapman Pond/4.1.13	66	1.2	0.9	Natural	3.2	Unknown	192	6.94	10.64	15
Clarkeville Pond/2.2.5	5	4	1.8	Manmade	1.4	M,D,Sl	75	6.70	8.10	25

Table 1. - Continued

Water Body/Station	Area (ha)	Max. depth (m)	Mean depth (m)	Basin	Shoreline (km)	Substrate	Conductivity (µS)	pH	DO (mg/l)	Water Temp. (°C)
Diamond Hill Res./1.5.11	104	-	5.2	Manmade	6.4	G,S,C	113	7.04	9.80	12
Easton Pond/10.0.22	54	2.1	2.1	Manmade	3.2	Unknown	224	8.19	9.25	21.5
Echo Lake, Barrington/9.b.23	2	1.4	0.5	Manmade	0.7	M	421	8.47	11.80	19.2
Echo Lake (Pascoag Res.)/1.4.2	142	5.8	3.4	Manmade	14.1	S,B,C,G	67	5.60	10.00	15
Eight Rod Farm Pond/9.b.54	2.4	4.8	1.5	Manmade	1	G,S	66	6.82	8.14	31
Eisenhower Lake/4.2.2	23	3.7	1.5	Manmade	4	D,M,B,C	42	6.71	10.50	14
Flat R. Res. (Johnson Pond)/3.3.6	267	11	2.6	Manmade	44.7	S,D,G	92	6.70	9.30	17.8
Fresh Pond/10.0.24	8	7.3	3.4	Natural	1.5	S	142	4.60	9.37	24.5
Georgiaville Pond/5.0.4	37	7.6	4	Manmade	4.1	D,M	160	8.00	9.00	25.8
Gorton Pond/9.a.2	25	13.7	4.9	Manmade	2	Unknown	254	9.21	11.13	21
Harrisville Mill Pond/1.4.4	4	3.4	1.7	Manmade	1.4	S,Sl,D	88	6.12	8.70	19.9
Hundred Acre Pond/4.3.4	34	11	5.5	Natural	3.2	C,G,S,D,M	84	6.79	9.80	19.5
Indian Lake/8.0.1	90	2.7	2.1	Manmade	4.4	B,C	161	6.03	9.37	18.3
Indian Run Res./8.0.13	3	-	-	Manmade	1	Unknown	174	5.94	8.75	13.1
J.L. Curran Res./3.2.29	12	5.2	3	Manmade	1.8	B,C	108	7.20	10.80	12.5
Keech Pond/1.3.9	52	4.3	1.4	Manmade	3.9	S,B,G,C	68	5.90	8.89	20
Killingly Pond/2.2.8	48	5.8	-	Manmade	4.2	B,G	35	5.00	8.80	17.3

Water Body/Station	Area (ha)	Max. depth (m)	Mean depth (m)	Basin	Shoreline (km)	Substrate	Conductivity (µS)	pH	DO (mg/l)	Water Temp. (°C)
Lake Washington/2.2.1	17	2.3	1.8	Manmade	1.9	Sl,D	110	6.30	10.40	15
Larkin Pond/4.3.3	18	10.4	4.3	Natural	1.1	S,G,D,M	89	7.05	10.30	14
Lawton Valley Reservoir/9.c.26	33	6.7	4.5	Manmade	3.5	Unknown	197	8.17	10.99	18.9
Lewis Farm Pond/10.0.23	<1	-	-	Natural	1.5	Sl	149	6.14	8.37	27
Little Pond/9.a.44	10	6.1	3.7	Natural	1.4	S,C,G	80	7.46	9.70	23
Locustville Pond/4.2.9	34	3.7	2.4	Manmade	5	G,S,D,M	57	6.90	7.56	28.5
Mashapaug Pond/3.1.6	28	5.2	2.1	Natural	3.7	Unknown	392	8.55	9.15	23.3
Meadow Brook Pond/4.1.14	2	2.5	1.2	Manmade	0.6	S,D,G	65	6.01	8.51	23.3
Melville Pond/9.c.28	3	10.1	3.7	Manmade	0.8	Unknown	279	7.04	9.26	27.4
Meshanticut Pond/3.1.5	3	3	1.5	Manmade	0.9	Unknown	472	9.76	13.70	26.7
Mishnock Pond/3.3.3	19	5.5	2.4	Natural	2.9	S,G,Sl,D,M	280	7.09	10.60	16
Nonquit Pond/9.b.25	82	3.5	2.4	Manmade	6.7	Unknown	107	5.93	8.59	15.8
Oak Swamp Reservoir/3.1.3	47	3	1.5	Manmade	4.7	B,S,Sl,D,M	146	7.47	9.20	21
Olney Pond/6.0.2	49	4.6	2.4	Manmade	5.8	S,M,D	230	7.60	9.55	19.5
Omega Pond/9.b.43	12	3.9	2.7	Manmade	2.1	Unknown	310	7.19	9.56	17
Pausacaco Pond/10.0.9	27	6.7	2.4	Manmade	2.6	Unknown	180	6.74	10.60	18.4
Peck Pond/2.2.6	5	4.3	1.5	Manmade	1.6	Sl,D,M	30	5.50	7.90	21
Plain Pond/4.2.26	2	4	-	Natural	0.5	M,G,S,D,C	34	4.00	7.84	28.5
Quidnick Reservoir/3.3.5	69	11	3.7	Manmade	4.7	C,S	104	6.46	9.85	17.5

Table 1. - Continued

Water Body/Station	Area (ha)	Max. depth (m)	Mean depth (m)	Basin	Shoreline (km)	Substrate	Conductivity (µS)	pH	DO (mg/l)	Water Temp. (°C)
Roger Williams Park Ponds/3.1.1	42	2.4	1.5	Manmade	6.7	Unknown	398	9.77	12.90	15.6
Saugatucket Pond/8.0.2	12	3.7	2.7	Manmade	2.7	M	107	6.22	9.03	18
Secret Lake/9.a.52	16	3.1	1.1	Manmade	3.4	Unknown	159	6.15	9.42	15
Shippee Saw Mill Pond/3.2.3	3	1.5	0.6	Manmade	0.7	B,D,M	50	6.21	9.00	22.2
Silver Spring Lake/10.0.10	7	4	1.5	Manmade	2.4	Unknown	152	6.56	9.22	23.4
Simmons Mill Pond/10.0.13	8	1.9	1.5	Manmade	1.8	Unknown	116	4.96	6.37	24.5
Slack Res./5.0.3	56	4.6	2.7	Manmade	6.1	S,Sl,D,M	143	7.21	8.10	20
Smith & Sayles Res./1.3.5	75	3.4	1.5	Manmade	7	B,D,M	66	5.86	8.90	22
Spring Green Pond/9.a.53	3.4	6.7	2.1	Manmade	1.3	D,M	204	6.36	6.50	22
Spring Lake (Herring Pond)/1.4.1	39	6.4	3	Natural	3.8	M	44	6.23	10.80	11.5
Stafford Pond/9.b.27	193	7.9	3	Natural	7.9	B,C,G,S	112	6.59	9.80	19.4
Tarbox Pond/3.3.4	12	2.1	2.1	Manmade	2.7	B,S,Sl,D,M	51	5.33	9.50	16.7
Tiogue Lake/3.3.2	87	3.4	1.8	Manmade	6.7	S	264	7.36	10.30	13.5
Tucker Pond/4.3.2	41	9.8	3.4	Natural	3.4	Unknown	42	5.87	6.65	23.5
Turner Reservoir/9.b.20	94	3.4	1.5	Manmade	3.4	Unknown	355	8.30	13.23	16.5
Upper Simmons Res.3.1.4	18	2.4	1.5	Manmade	2.3	Unknown	577	7.74	9.40	23

Table 1. - Continued

Water Body/Station	Area (ha)	Max. depth (m)	Mean depth (m)	Basin	Shoreline (km)	Substrate	Conductivity (µS)	pH	DO (mg/l)	Water Temp. (°C)
Upper Slatersville Res./1.2.7	56	7	2.4	Manmade	7.3	Sl	86	6.81	9.80	17
Wakefield Pond/2.2.2	29	6.4	1.8	Manmade	4.3	Sl,G,S	31	5.90	9.50	19.5
Wallum Lake/1.4.3	130	22.6	8.5	Natural	8.7	B,C,G,S	38	6.35	10.90	22.8
Warwick Pond/9.a.3	34	7.9	4.3	Natural	2.6	Unknown	203	9.41	12.50	24.5
Watchaug Pond/4.1.15	232	11	2.4	Natural	7.9	S,G	59	5.73	9.20	18.6
Waterman Res./5.0.2	124	4.6	2.1	Manmade	11.2	C,S	90	6.91	8.80	23.8
Watson Reservoir/9.b.24	152	6.1	-	Manmade	5.5	B,C,G,Sl	135	6.34	7.12	18.3
Wenscott Res./6.0.1	32	3.4	2.1	Manmade	3.5	Sl,D	126	7.60	9.50	18
Wesquage Pond/9.a.41	22	1.8	1	Natural	2.7	S	3130			17
Wilson Reservoir/1.4.5	45	4	2.1	Manmade	4.4	C,G	71	4.70	9.00	18
Wincheck Pond/4.2.3	54	7.3	2.1	Manmade	5.2	B,C,D,G,M	41	4.73	10.10	16.5
Woonasquatucket Res./5.0.5	123	4.6	2.7	Manmade	12.2	Unknown	150	7.49	8.02	24.1
Worden Pond/4.3.1	420	2.1	1.2	Natural	9.8	S,Sl,C,G,B,D	77	6.45	8.70	19
Wyoming Pond/4.2.8	12	4	2.7	Manmade	2.2	Unknown	91	6.36	9.21	24.5
Yawgoo Pond/4.4.1	55	11.3	2.7	Manmade	3	G,S,D,Sl,C	54	7.05	9.05	20.5
Yawgoog Pond/4.2.1	66	7.9	4.9	Manmade	4.6	D,Bd,B,G,S	37	4.41	11.20	12.5

Results and Discussion

Three hundred and seventy-seven localities (92 ponds and 285 stream segments) were surveyed between 1993 and 2007 (Figure 13). The majority of ponds were manmade (Table 1), and were formed, for the most part, by the damming of rivers and streams. Many are choked with rooted, submersed aquatic macrophytes such as water milfoil and by rooted, floating-leafed varieties like water lilies. Because of the shallow nature of these ponds, light is able to penetrate through the water column to the bottom, stimulating plant growth. Lotic environments varied from cool, shaded, moderately flowing headwater streams to warmer, slower flowing mainstems of large rivers fully exposed to sunlight. Eight localities, one pond and seven stream locations, were influenced by the rise and fall of the tide. Salinities at these locations varied widely, depending on the stage of the tide.

Seventy-two species of fish, representing 34 families, were collected (Table 2). These fish can be grouped into three categories: (1) fish that live entirely in freshwater but may occasionally stray into brackish water, (2) fish that migrate regularly between freshwater and saltwater as part of their reproductive cycle (collectively referred to as being diadromous), and (3) fish that move back and forth, regularly or intermittently, between saltwater and freshwater but are not diadromous. The majority of species in this group, such as those found in the families Fundulidae (topminnows), Carangidae (jacks), and Syngnathidae (pipefishes), were collected in tidal areas.

Endangered species (federal or state) were not collected. However, the Rhode Island Natural Heritage Program has listed the American brook lamprey as state threatened because of the likelihood of it becoming endangered in the future if current trends in habitat loss remain unchanged.

Fish were not found in several locations; five streams and one pond (Figure 14). Since dissolved oxygen concentrations (1.90 to 14.23 ppm), pH (3.90 to 9.77), temperature (4 to 28.5° C), and conductivity (29.5 to 3440µ S) were within ranges measured elsewhere where fish were collected (Table 3), it is believed that these parameters were not limiting factors. Although flowing during the time of the survey, it is possible that some of these streams are intermittent and may occasionally go dry during extreme droughts, forcing any fish that may have been present to move to refuges located downstream. Dams, falls, or culverts that restrict the upstream movement of fish could have prevented recolonization when water flows returned to normal. Among three locations sampled on the Pocasset River, one did not contain fish. The substrate at this station, located between two stations where fish were collected, was covered with an orange flocculent-like substance that probably consisted of iron bacteria. The flocculent may have created unsuitable habitat for fish in this reach of the river. Although fish were not collected in Plain Pond, a small kettle pond that was formed during the glacial retreat, aquatic insects and tadpoles were observed.

Thirty-two species of freshwater fish, representing 21 native and 11 introduced or nonindigenous species, were collected (Table 2). All of the native freshwater species that were collected are found in the neighboring states of Connecticut and Massachusetts (Whitworth 1996; Hartel et al. 2002). Natives species, such as the pumpkinseed, chain pickerel, brook trout, brown bullhead, and golden shiner were among the most widely distributed species collected (Table 4).

The introduction of nonindigenous species began in 1870 with the stocking of

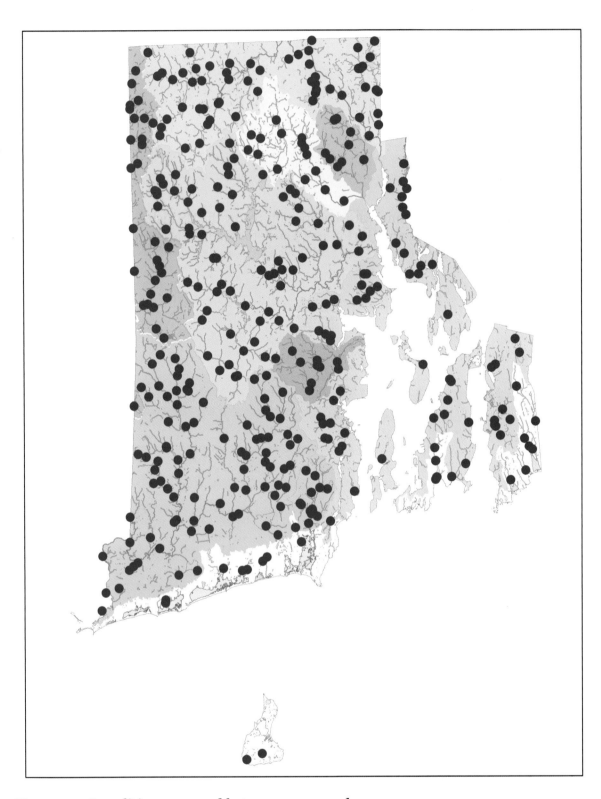

Figure 13. Localities surveyed between 1993 and 2007.

smallmouth bass (CIF 1872). By the turn of the century, four more nonindigenous species were introduced into the state's freshwaters, the common carp, goldfish, largemouth bass, and brown trout (CIF 1881,1891,1895,1896). Bluegill and rainbow trout were introduced later in 1914 and 1916, respectively (CIF 1915; CIF 1917). Largemouth bass and bluegill were among the most widely distributed fish collected (Table 4).

Many nonindigenous species have been stocked over the years which appear not to have become naturalized. These include brown trout, rainbow trout, northern pike, rock bass (*Ambloplites rupestris*), and channel catfish (*Ictalurus punctatus*). Brown trout, rainbow trout, and northern pike are stocked periodically by the state for its "put-and-take" fishery. The rock bass that were first reported in the early 1900s on Aquidneck Island are believed to have been introduced (Tracy 1910). Rock bass were never collected during the present survey. Channel catfish were cultured by the US Fish & Wildlife Service at the Arcadia Hatchery (Saila and Horton 1957) and stocked in at least two locations, Ashville and Yawgoog Ponds (Guthrie and Stolgitis 1977).

Although spottail shiners (*Notropis hudsonius*) were reported to have been collected in the Ashaway River and at one location in the Pawcatuck River by Guthrie et al. (1973), they were never collected during the present survey. Since large river systems, such as the Connecticut, Merrimack, and Housatonic Rivers, are the preferred habitat for this species (Whitworth et al. 1968; Jenkins and Burkhead 1993; Hartel et al. 2002), it is possible that the spottail shiners that were collected by Guthrie et al. were not indigenous but were baitfish introductions that had not become naturalized.

Native species, such as the brook trout and white perch, were also widely stocked throughout the state. The purpose of all introductions was to bolster native fish populations to provide more food and game opportunities for the angler.

Ten diadromous species were collected. The majority (9) of these fish were anadromous (Table 2). North America's only catadromous species, the American eel, was the most widely distributed species collected (Page 50), occurring in nearly 53 percent of the locations sampled.

Among the anadromous species collected, the alewife was the most widely distributed (Page 60), occurring in nine percent of the locations sampled (Table 4). The population of alewives in Omega Pond, an impoundment at the mouth of the Ten Mile River, is maintained by volunteers who catch them in nets below the pond's dam. Volunteers have been transporting alewives over the dam each spring since at least the 1970s. Landlocked populations were documented in Hundred Acre Pond, Beach Pond, and Wallum Lake. The alewives documented in Hundred Acre Pond were first reported in the 1950s by Saila and Horten (1957). Those collected in Beach Pond and Wallum Lake became established in the 1980s when adults were stocked to provide forage for a program to grow trophy-sized trout. This program was unsuccessful and discontinued (Lapin 1992).

American shad, adult and young-of-the-year, were collected from several locations in the lower Pawcatuck River (Page 64). Hickory shad (adults), on the other hand, were collected from one location near the mouth of the Pawcatuck River near Avondale (Page 66). Since spawning for this anadromous species occurs in rivers from Maryland to Florida, it generally remains in coastal waters and does not venture very far into freshwater again during its seasonal migration north. Anglers in Rhode Island frequently catch hickory shad on artificial lures during the summer in a number of coastal areas.

Atlantic salmon were collected throughout the Pawcatuck River watershed (Page

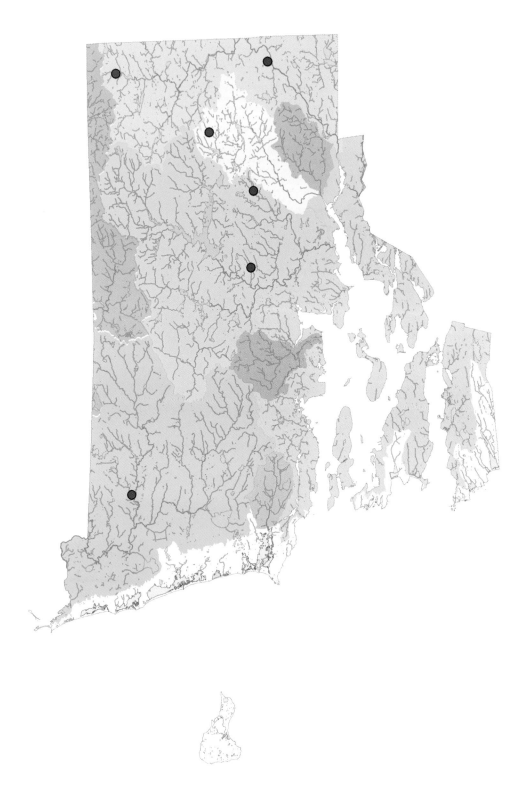

Figure 14. Localities where fish were not collected.

Results and Discussion

128). Except for adult salmon that are collected at the Potter Hill Dam fishway, all other locations contained young that had been stocked earlier by the Division in an attempt to restore a self-sustaining population to this river system. The Atlantic salmon that were collected in the Hunt River watershed were the result of a one-time stocking of surplus salmon parr in 1996. Salmon have not been collected in the Hunt River in subsequent surveys.

Small sea lampreys, approximately 12 inches (305 mm) in length, are occasionally found attached to adult American shad that are returning to the Pawcatuck River to spawn (Page 46). It is believed that no spawning populations occur in Rhode Island's freshwaters as no adult sea lampreys were ever collected. Spawning populations are found in Connecticut and Massachusetts (Whitworth 1996; Hartel et al. 2002).

Anadromous fish runs once occurred more widely in Rhode Island than they do now. Atlantic salmon and American shad runs, for example, were once found in the Pawtuxet and Blackstone Rivers before the construction of impassible dams that prevented them from ascending these rivers to spawn (CIF 1872; Buckley and Nixon 2001).

Twenty-nine species of fish that regularly or occasionally spend a portion of their lives in both fresh and saltwater were collected (Table 2). Most were collected in an area in the lower Pawcatuck River below the head-of-tide (Figure 2). A few in this group appear to be residents while others appear to be transients, appearing only during the summer and fall months. Residents included species that belong to such families as Gasterosteidae (sticklebacks), Pleuronectidae (righteye flounders), and Fundulidae (topminnows).

Transients generally consisted of the juvenile life stages of certain warmwater species, belonging to such families as Carangidae (jacks), Clupeidae (herrings), or Mugilidae (mullets) that use estuarine waters as nursery areas during the summer. Large numbers of juvenile Atlantic menhaden, a transient in the family Clupeidae, were regularly collected in the lower Pawcatuck River during the late summer and fall. Adult menhaden are commonly found in coastal regions throughout the summer. When water temperatures drop in the fall these transients generally move down the coast to warmer waters. Many of the species in this group were also collected during surveys of Rhode Island's coastal ponds, tidal rivers, and embayments (Satchwill 2003).

The American eel and the largemouth bass were the most commonly occurring fish species, appearing in more than half of the localities sampled (Table 4), in all ten of the state's watersheds (Table 5), and in both stream and pond locations (Table 6). Pumpkinseed, bluegill, chain pickerel, brook trout, and brown bullhead were also widely distributed, appearing in more than a third of the localities sampled and at least nine of the state's ten drainage basins. Collections of such species as the American brook lamprey and the American shad were limited in their distribution.

A few interesting patterns were noted in the geographical distribution of several species. American brook lampreys, for example, were only found in the northeastern part of the State in the Blackstone River drainage basin (Page 44). They are also found in Massachusetts, particularly in the Blackstone River drainage (Hartel et al. 2002). Redbreast sunfish, on the other hand, were only collected in the western areas of the state from the Moosup River, south to the lower Pawcatuck and Wood River drainages (Page 198). The redbreast sunfish was not collected in the Pawcatuck River watershed above Shannock Falls on the Richmond-Charlestown border. The falls may have acted as a natural barrier to redbreast sunfish recolonizing the Pawcatuck after the glacial retreat. Redbreast sunfish are widely distributed in the neighboring states of Connecticut and Massachusetts (Whitworth et al. 1968;

Hartel et al. 2002).

Although widely dispersed throughout the state, the distribution of the American eel was limited to just a few locations in the Blackstone and Pawtuxet River drainages (Page 50). Dams located in these drainages have undoubtedly impeded the upstream migration of this catadromous species. Since eels have the ability to leave the water and writhe over obstructions blocking their upstream migration, they are occasionally encountered in the upper reaches of the Blackstone. Numerous fish surveys conducted in Wilson Reservoir and Echo Lake show that a very limited number of eels are succesfully migrating into the upper reaches of the Blackstone River drainage. Although somewhat widely dispersed throughout the state, the tessellated darter was conspicuously absent in the Hunt and Pawtuxet River drainages (Page 214). The distributions of such species as the northern pike, and the brown and rainbow trout is determined, for the most part, by stocking locations.

Preferences for lotic and lentic habitat were noted for a number of species (Table 6). For example, species such as the Atlantic salmon, blacknose dace, and longnose dace were caught exclusively in streams. Brook trout were collected, for the most part, from streams, most of which were cool and well-oxygenated. Wild brook trout were not collected in ponds. However, there were a number of streams and ponds where stocked brook trout were collected. Salmonids are stocked periodically throughout the state by the Division for its put-and-take fisheries. Largemouth bass, pumpkinseed, golden shiner, and yellow perch were collected in a greater proportion of ponds than streams. Ponds or the quiet areas of streams and rivers are the preferred habitat for these species. Generally, it was the juveniles of these specics that were collected in the lotic environment, utilizing the streams as a means of dispersal. The American eel was commonly found in both ponds and streams.

Species diversity or richness can be defined as the variety or number of species found in a given area. The diversity of fish in freshwater systems can be affected by such factors as the introduction of non-native species, dam construction, the number of physiographic regions, and by such hydrographic features as the size of the drainage basin, and stream order. Stream order is a measure of the relative size of a stream that is based on the number of tributaries flowing into it from upstream areas (see glossary). In the present survey, diversity was generally found to increase with an increase in stream order (Table 7). Two of the state's largest drainages, the Pawcatuck and Blackstone River basins, contained the greatest diversity of fish, 67 and 31 species, respectively. The large variety of fish collected in the Pawcatuck River can be attributed, for the most part, to where the surveys were conducted in the rivers. In the Pawcatuck, several stations were located in areas below the head-of-tide where there were no obstructions inhibiting the movement of fish from the marine environment, whereas in the Blackstone, all surveys were conducted in areas above tidal influence and where dams blocked the upstream movement of fish (anadromous and marine) from Narragansett Bay.

This report contains information on fish that were collected between 1993 and 2007. Since then, five new species of fish have been discovered, see update on page 37.

Table 2. - Fish species collected during the 1993-2007 Stream & Pond Survey. Classification abbreviations: A = anadromous, C = catadromous, F = freshwater (n = native, i = introduced), and M = marine. * Anadromous populations found elsewhere.

Family		
Common Name	*Scientific name*	**Classification**
Petromyzontidae - lampreys		
American brook lamprey	*Lampetra appendix*	F (n)
sea lamprey	*Petromyzon marinus*	A
Anguillidae - freshwater eels		
American eel	*Anguilla rostrata*	C
Engraulidae - anchovies		
bay anchovy	*Anchoa mitchilli*	M, F
Clupeidae - herrings		
blueback herring	*Alosa aestivalis*	A
hickory shad	*Alosa mediocris*	A
alewife	*Alosa pseudoharengus*	A
American shad	*Alosa sapidissima*	A
Atlantic menhaden	*Brevoortia tyrannus*	M, F
gizzard shad	*Dorsoma cepedianum*	F (n) *
Cyprinidae - carps and minnows		
goldfish	*Carassius auratus*	F (i)
common carp	*Cyprinus carpio*	F (i)
common shiner	*Luxilus cornutus*	F (n)
golden shiner	*Notemigonus crysoleucas*	F (n)
bridle shiner	*Notropis bifrenatus*	F (n)
blacknose dace	*Rhinichthys atratulus*	F (n)
longnose dace	*Rhinichthys cataractae*	F (n)
fallfish	*Semotilus corporalis*	F (n)
Catostomidae - suckers		
white sucker	*Catostomus commersoni*	F (n)
creek chubsucker	*Erimyzon oblongus*	F (n)

Table 2 continued.

Family		
Common Name	*Scientific name*	**Classification**
Ictaluridae - North American catfishes		
white catfish	*Ameiurus catus*	F (i)
yellow bullhead	*Ameiurus natalis*	F (i)
brown bullhead	*Ameiurus nebulosus*	F (n)
Esocidae - pikes		
redfin pickerel	*Esox americanus americanus*	F (n)
northern pike	*Esox lucius*	F (i)
chain pickerel	*Esox niger*	F (n)
Osmeridae - smelts		
rainbow smelt	*Osmerus mordax*	A
Salmonidae - trouts and salmons		
rainbow trout	*Oncorhynchus mykiss*	F (i) *
Atlantic salmon	*Salmo salar*	A
brown trout	*Salmo trutta*	F (i) *
brook trout	*Salvelinus fontinalis*	F (n) *
Gadidae - cods		
Atlantic tomcod	*Microgadus tomcod*	M, F
Mugilidae - mullets		
white mullet	*Mugil curema*	M, F
Atherinopsidae - New World silversides		
Atlantic silverside	*Menidia menidia*	M
inland silverside	*Menidia beryllina*	M, F
Belonidae - needlefishes		
Atlantic needlefish	*Strongylura marina*	M, F

Table 2 continued.

Family		
Common Name	*Scientific name*	**Classification**
Fundulidae - topminnows		
banded killifish	*Fundulus diaphanus*	F (n)
mummichog	*Fundulus heteroclitus*	M, F
striped killifish	*Fundulus majalis*	M
rainwater killifish	*Lucania parva*	M, F
Cyprinodontidae - pupfishes		
sheepshead minnow	*Cyprinodon variegatus*	M, F
Gasterosteidae - sticklebacks		
fourspine stickleback	*Apeltes quadracus*	M, F
threespine stickleback	*Gasterosteus aculeatus*	A
ninespine stickleback	*Pungitius pungitius*	M, F
Syngnathidae - pipefishes		
northern pipefish	*Syngnathus fuscus*	M
Triglidae - searobins		
northern searobin	*Prionotus carolinus*	M
Moronidae - temperate basses		
white perch	*Morone americana*	M, F
striped bass	*Morone saxatilis*	A
Centrarchidae - sunfishes		
banded sunfish	*Enneacanthus obesus*	F (n)
redbreast sunfish	*Lepomis auritus*	F (n)
pumpkinseed	*Lepomis gibbosus*	F (n)
bluegill	*Lepomis macrochirus*	F (i)
smallmouth bass	*Micropterus dolomieu*	F (i)
largemouth bass	*Micropterus salmoides*	F (i)
black crappie	*Pomoxis nigromaculatus*	F (i)

Table 2 continued.

Family		
Common Name	*Scientific name*	**Classification**
Percidae - perches		
swamp darter	*Etheostoma fusiforme*	F (n)
tessellated darter	*Etheostoma olmstedi*	F (n)
yellow perch	*Perca flavescens*	F (n)
Pomatomidae - bluefishes		
bluefish	*Pomatomus saltatrix*	M
Carangidae - jacks		
crevalle jack	*Caranx hippos*	M
lookdown	*Selene vomer*	M
Lutjanidae - snappers		
gray snapper	*Lutjanus griseus*	M, F
Gerreidae - mojarras		
spotfin mojarra	*Eucinostomus argenteus*	M, F
Labridae - wrasses		
tautog	*Tautoga onitis*	M
Sparidae - porgies		
pinfish	*Lagodon rhomboides*	M, F
Sciaenidae - drums		
weakfish	*Cynoscion regalis*	M
northern kingfish	*Menticirrhus saxatilis*	M
Gobiidae - gobies		
naked goby	*Gobiosoma bosc*	M, F
Stromateidae - butterfishes		
butterfish	Peprilus triacanthus	M

Table 2 continued.

Family		
Common Name	*Scientific name*	**Classification**
Scophthalmidae - turbots		
windowpane	*Scophthalmus aquosus*	M
Pleuronectidae - righteye flounders		
winter flounder	*Pseudopleuronectes americanus*	M
Achiridae - American soles		
hogchoker	*Trinectes maculatus*	M, F

Table 3. - Number of observations (N), mean and (range) by fish species, of the chemical parameters measured during the 1993-2007 Stream & Pond Survey when electrofishing.

Fish Species	N	pH	Water Temperature (°C)	Dissolved Oxygen (mg/l)	Conductivity (µS)
alewife*	37	7.03 (5.50-9.41)	19.93 (10.0-28.5)	8.95 (5.44-12.5)	449.7 (38-3440)
American brook lamprey	7	6.50 (6.14-7.04)	15.6 (4-21)	7.68 (4.9-10.0)	174 (114-245)
American eel*	231	6.55 (3.90-9.76)	19.8 (8-33)	8.42 (1.90-14.23)	209.6 (31-43800)
American shad*	1	6.64	24	7.05	179
Atlantic menhaden*	1	6.28	16.9	6.86	374
Atlantic salmon	29	6.31 (5.58-6.88)	18.3 (11-23.2)	8.67 (7.34-10.18)	84.8 (33-252)
Atlantic tomcod*	1	6.28	16.9	6.86	374
banded killifish*	38	6.63 (5.50-8.00)	19.2 (9-28)	8.82 (2.51-13.48)	258.7 (30-3440)
banded sunfish	36	5.99 (4.50-6.60)	19.5 (4-25.4)	7.81 (2.64-10.90)	99.1 (22-263)
black crappie	65	6.82 (4.96-9.77)	18.7 (5-27.4)	9.18 (5.1-13.23)	245 (64-3440)
blacknose dace	13	6.51 (5.80-7.18)	18.8 (14.2-21)	8.56 (6.8-11.94)	137.5 (33-443)
blueback herring*	4	6.95 (6.22-7.90)	19.35 (16-25)	9.40 (9.03-10.06)	212.8 (107-392)
bluegill*	167	6.65 (4.40-9.77)	19.7 (9-28.5)	8.89 (4.69-13.70)	186.7 (29.5-3440)
bridle shiner	12	6.32 (5.71-6.70)	20.24 (13.00-28.00)	9.25 (8.68-10.05)	87 (22-184)
brook trout	155	6.27 (4.35-7.60)	18.2 (9-24)	8.48 (3.75-14.23)	120 (30-761)
brown trout*	33	6.44 (4.96-8.62)	20.00 (12.4-28.5)	8.88 (6.37-10.90)	228.3 (51-3440)
brown bullhead	164	6.45 (4.41-9.76)	19.6 (5-33)	8.56 (4.20-13.70)	164.7 (27-3440)
chain pickerel*	184	6.42 (4.40-9.76)	19.8 (5-33)	8.50 (3.70-13.70)	150.4 (22-3440)
common carp	22	7.67 (6.23-9.77)	20.3 (12.2-28)	9.51 (5.1-13.70)	639.6 (126-3440)
common shiner	27	6.52 (5.63-7.90)	19.0 (11-28)	8.46 (5.10-11.00)	165.8 (48-601)
creek chubsucker	29	6.22 (4.75-7.66)	20.2 (15-28.5)	8.28 (4.69-10.20)	101.4 (30-393)
fallfish	58	6.40 (5.15-7.90)	20.1 (8-28)	8.07 (4.85-12.43)	131.5 (45-460)
fourspine stickleback*	7	6.60 (6.15-7.07)	20.01 (18.8-21)	6.73 (1.90-13.48)	358.1 (142-773)

Table 3. – Continued

Fish Species	N	pH	Water Temperature (°C)	Dissolved Oxygen (mg/l)	Conductivity (µS)
gizzard shad*	6	7.92 (6.64-9.41)	24 (17-28)	9.40 (7.05-12.50)	903 (179-2090)
golden shiner*	142	6.57 (3.90-9.77)	19.7 (5-33)	8.55 (1.90-13.70)	209.2 (30-3440)
goldfish	2	7.07	18.3 (16-20.5)	7.92	496
inland silverside*	3	6.72 (6.28-7.07)	20.8 (16.9-25)	7.83 (6.86-8.91)	670 (374-1140)
largemouth bass*	239	6.61 (4.41-9.77)	20.1 (5-33)	8.68 (4.20-13.70)	196.7 (29.5-3440)
longnose dace	31	6.54 (5.78-7.76)	19.7 (14-26)	8.34 (4.90-11.66)	174.0 (42-471)
mummichog*	11	6.41 (5.25-7.07)	18.2 (10-21)	7.87 (3.67-13.48)	542.8 (66-3130)
ninespine stickleback	11	6.47 (5.88-7.05)	18.9 (15-21.1)	7.44 (1.90-14.23)	301.6 (158-468)
northern pike	8	6.40 (5.54-6.94)	18.1 (8-23.3)	9.09 (5.10-12.43)	188.6 (67-601)
pumpkinseed*	225	6.59 (4.15-9.77)	19.6 (5-33)	8.61 (1.90-13.70)	202.4 (22-2440)
rainbow trout*	31	6.22 (4.96-7.60)	20.2 (12.4-24.7)	8.76 (6.37-10.90)	113.0 (38-372)
rainwater killifish*	1		10		3130
redbreast sunfish*	16	6.47 (5.78-6.94)	20.8 (15-28.5)	8.29 (6.09-10.64)	109.1 (54-211)
redfin pickerel	125	6.22 (3.90-7.76)	19.3 (13-26.1)	7.81 (2.63-11.66)	162.8 (31-2250)
smallmouth bass	15	6.62 (5.73-7.47)	18.6 (12.2-25)	9.01 (5.48-10.30)	152.2 (59-329)
swamp darter	47	6.20 (4.75-7.09)	19.8 (5-31.5)	8.35 (4.00-12.42)	117.8 (22-280)
tessellated darter	89	6.44 (4.70-7.90)	20.1 (11-26.9)	8.12 (4.20-11.66)	160.6 (39-773)
threespine stickleback*	3	6.84 (6.15-7.54)	20.8 (19.5-22)	5.14 (1.90-7.28)	378 (211-498)
white catfish	13	6.87 (5.71-8.30)	18.8 (8-24.7)	9.38 (7.05-13.23)	207.6 (39-442)
white perch*	64	7.08 (5.60-9.77)	19.4 (8-28.5)	9.16 (5.10-13.23)	301.8 (42-3130)
white sucker*	141	6.53 (4.70-9.21)	19.4 (9-28.5)	8.44 (4.85-13.23)	164.5 (42-773)
yellow bullhead	34	7.19 (6.11-9.76)	20.6 (5-28)	9.10 (5.10-13.70)	248.2 (62-601)
yellow perch*	144	6.62 (4.41-9.77)	19.4 (5-33)	9.04 (4.70-13.23)	183.4 (30-3440)

*Also collected during supplementary sampling in areas where salinities were as high as 25 ppt.

Table 4. - Number (total of 377) and percentage of locations where a species of fish was collected during the 1993-2007 Stream & Pond Survey.

Fish Species	Locations	
	Number	Percentage
American eel	198	52.5
largemouth bass	193	51.2
pumpkinseed	181	48.0
bluegill	159	42.2
chain pickerel	153	40.6
brook trout	140	37.1
brown bullhead	140	37.1
golden shiner	120	31.8
redfin pickerel	118	31.3
white sucker	116	30.8
yellow perch	114	30.2
tessellated darter	79	21.0
fallfish	53	14.1
white perch	50	13.3
black crappie	48	12.2
swamp darter	43	11.4
banded sunfish	40	10.6
banded killifish	39	10.3
alewife	35	9.3
brown trout	32	8.5
yellow bullhead	31	8.2
rainbow trout	29	7.7
creek chubsucker	27	7.2
Atlantic salmon	26	6.9
longnose dace	26	6.9
common shiner	20	5.3
redbreast sunfish	16	4.2
common carp	15	4.0
mummichog	15	4.0
white catfish	15	4.0
blacknose dace	13	3.4
smallmouth bass	13	3.4
ninespine stickleback	12	3.2
bridle shiner	10	2.7

Table 4 continued.

Fish Species	Locations	
	Number	Percentage
fourspine stickleback	9	2.4
gizzard shad	7	1.9
inland silverside	7	1.9
American brook lamprey	6	1.6
northern pike	6	1.6
blueback herring	5	1.3
threespine stickleback	5	1.3
American shad	4	1.1
sheepshead minnow	4	1.1
Atlantic menhaden	3	0.8
striped bass	3	0.8
Atlantic silverside	2	0.5
Atlantic tomcod	2	0.5
goldfish	2	0.5
rainwater killifish	2	0.5
striped killifish	2	0.5
hickory shad	1	0.3

Table 5. - Occurrence, by drainage basin, of fish species collected during the 1993 - 2007 Stream & Pond Survey.

Fish species	Drainage Basin									
	Black-stone River	Thames River	Pawtuxet River	Pawcatuck River	Wooasqua-tucket River	Moshas-suck River	Hunt River	Saug-atucket River	Narra-gansett Bay	Atlantic Ocean
alewife	•	•		•	•		•	•	•	•
American brook lamprey	•									
American eel	•	•	•	•	•	•	•	•	•	•
American shad				•						
Atlantic menhaden				•					•	
Atlantic salmon				•			•			
Atlantic tomcod				•						
banded killifish	•	•		•	•	•		•	•	•
banded sunfish	•	•	•	•			•		•	•
black crappie	•	•	•	•	•	•		•	•	•
blacknose dace	•	•	•	•	•	•				
blueback herring				•			•			
bluegill	•	•	•	•	•	•	•	•	•	•
bridle shiner	•	•	•	•						•
brook trout	•	•	•	•		•	•	•	•	•
brown trout	•	•	•	•		•		•		•
brown bullhead	•	•	•	•	•		•	•	•	•

Table 5. continued.

Drainage Basin

Fish species	Blackstone River	Thames River	Pawtuxet River	Pawcatuck River	Wooasquatucket River	Moshassuck River	Hunt River	Saugatucket River	Narragansett Bay	Atlantic Ocean
chain pickerel	•	•	•	•	•	•	•	•	•	•
common carp	•		•			•			•	
common shiner	•	•		•						
creek chubsucker	•	•	•	•	•	•				
fallfish	•	•	•	•	•					
fourspine stickleback									•	•
gizzard shad				•					•	
golden shiner	•	•	•	•	•	•	•	•	•	•
goldfish									•	
inland silverside				•					•	
largemouth bass	•	•	•	•	•	•	•	•	•	•
longnose dace	•	•	•			•	•			
mummichog				•						
ninespine stickleback										
northern pike	•			•	•				•	•
pumpkinseed	•	•	•	•	•	•	•	•	•	•
rainbow trout	•	•	•	•	•	•		•		•
rainwater killifish									•	

Table 5. continued.

	Drainage Basin									
Fish species	Blackstone River	Thames River	Pawtuxet River	Pawcatuck River	Wooasquatucket River	Moshassuck River	Hunt River	Saugatucket River	Narragansett Bay	Atlantic Ocean
redbreast sunfish		•		•						
redfin pickerel	•		•	•	•	•	•	•	•	•
sea lamprey				•						
sheepshead minnow				•					•	
smallmouth bass	•		•	•		•		•	•	
striped bass				•				•	•	
striped killifish				•					•	
swamp darter	•	•	•	•	•		•	•	•	•
tessellated darter	•	•		•	•	•		•	•	•
threespine stickleback				•						•
white catfish	•	•	•	•				•	•	
white perch	•	•	•	•	•	•			•	•
white sucker	•	•	•	•	•	•	•		•	
yellow bullhead	•		•		•	•			•	
yellow perch	•	•	•	•	•	•		•	•	•
other *				•						

* Species that were only collected in the lower Pawcatuck River: Atlantic needlefish, Atlantic silverside, bay anchovy, bluefish, butterfish, crevalle jack, gray snapper, hickory shad, hogchoker, lookdown, naked goby, northern kingfish, northern pipefish, northern searobin, pinfish, rainbow smelt, spotfin mojarra, tautog, weakfish, white mullet, windowpane, and winter flounder.

Table 6. - Percent occurrence, by stream and pond, of fish species collected during the 1993 - 2007 Stream and Pond Survey.

Fish Species	% Occurrence	
	Stream Locations	Pond Locations
alewife	6.3	18.5
American brook lamprey	2.1	0.0
American eel	47.7	66.3
American shad	1.4	0.0
Atlantic menhaden	1.1	0.0
Atlantic salmon	10.9	0.0
Atlantic silverside	0.4	0.0
Atlantic tomcod	0.7	0.0
banded killifish	4.9	30.1
banded sunfish	9.1	15.2
black crappie	3.5	39.1
blacknose dace	4.6	0.0
blueback herring	1.1	2.2
bluegill	28.4	84.8
bridle shiner	1.8	3.3
brook trout	46.7	7.6
brown bullhead	27.0	69.6
brown trout	6.0	16.3
chain pickerel	29.1	73.9
common carp	1.4	12.0
common shiner	7.0	1.1
creek chubsucker	6.0	12.1
fallfish	18.6	1.1
fourspine stickleback	3.2	0.0
gizzard shad	1.1	2.2
golden shiner	19.6	71.7
goldfish	0.4	1.1
hickory shad	0.4	0.0
inland silverside	1.4	1.1
largemouth bass	36.8	95.7
longnose dace	9.1	0.0
mummichog	4.9	1.1

Table 6. continued.

Fish Species	% Occurrence	
	Stream Locations	Pond Locations
ninespine stickleback	4.2	0.0
northern pike	0.7	4.3
pumpkinseed	33.7	87.0
rainbow trout	4.6	17.4
rainwater killifish	0.4	1.1
redbreast sunfish	3.9	4.3
redfin pickerel	39.3	5.4
sheepshead minnow	1.1	1.1
smallmouth bass	1.4	9.8
striped bass	1.1	0.0
striped killifish	0.7	0.0
swamp darter	7.7	26.1
tessellated darter	25.3	6.5
threespine stickleback	2.1	0.0
white catfish	3.2	5.4
white perch	3.9	41.3
white sucker	33.0	23.9
yellow bullhead	6.0	16.3
yellow perch	11.6	88.0

Table 7. - Mean number of species by stream order.

Stream Order	Mean No. of species	Range	SD	N
1	3.1	1-11	2.18	78
2	4.1	1-11	2.27	139
3	7.3	1-16	3.15	55
4	7.4	4-18	3.26	21
5	12.3	4-20	7.29	4

Update for 2008 to 2012

This publication is based on fish surveys that were conducted between 1993 and 2007. During the current 2008-2012 phase, the following native (*) and nonnative (**) species were identified for the first time in collections:

Species	Location
Guppy (*Poecilia reticulata*)**	Maidford River, Middletown
Rock bass (*Ambloplites rupestris*)**	Blackstone River, Valley Falls
Green sunfish (*Lepomis cyanellus*)**	Mill River, Woonsocket
Striped mullet (*Mugil cephalus*)*	Mattatuxet River, North Kingstown
Sea-run brook trout (*Salvelinus fontinalis*)*	North Kingstown and South Kingstown

Using this Publication as an Aid for Identifying Fish

1. Refer to General Anatomy, shown to the right, which illustrates the various structures that are commonly used to identify fish.

2. Carefully observe your fish, paying particular attention to the general shape of the body, the number, size, and placement of the fins, the shape and position of the mouth, the size of the scales, and if barbels are readily observable around the mouth.

3. Compare your fish with the black and white, and color illustrations in Species Accounts. Color is based on pictures of live fish or from newly collected specimens. Fish are not drawn to scale and therefore, all will appear to be of the same size. Refer to Family and Species Accounts for the characteristics that are commonly used for identification.

4. Refer to the distribution maps as they may sometimes be used to eliminate a species that was caught outside of an area where it is generally found.

General Anatomy

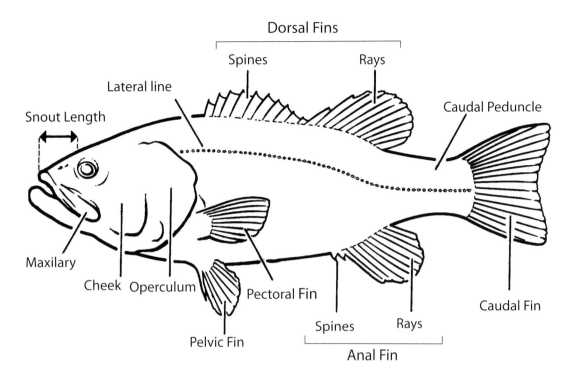

Dorsal Fins

Spines   Rays

Lateral line

Snout Length

Caudal Peduncle

Maxilary

Cheek   Operculum

Pectoral Fin

Pelvic Fin

Spines   Rays

Anal Fin

Caudal Fin

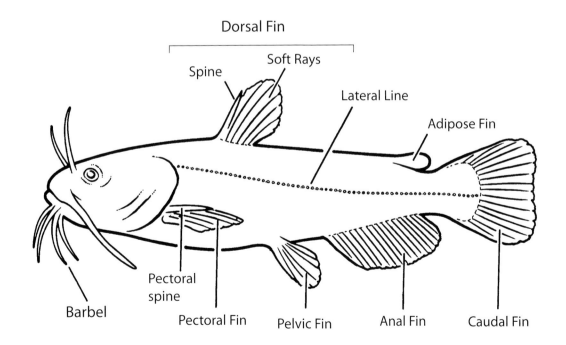

Dorsal Fin

Spine   Soft Rays

Lateral Line

Adipose Fin

Pectoral
spine

Barbel

Pectoral Fin   Pelvic Fin   Anal Fin   Caudal Fin

Family and Species Accounts
Introduction

Family accounts provide general information on the morphological characteristics that group closely related species together, the habitat in which it can be found and its geographical or worldwide distribution. Species accounts provide the common and scientific names of each species, the name(s) of the author(s) who first described the species (names within parentheses indicate that the species has been placed in another genus since its original description), a line drawing and color illustration for each species, and a map showing the locations where individuals were caught. Also discussed is whether a species is naturally occurring (native) or has been introduced (nonnative or exotic), a description of its general distribution in North America, a description of the habitat in which it was caught, a description of selected anatomical features and coloration to aid the reader in identification, and life history information. The range of environmental conditions (i.e., temperature, pH, oxygen, and conductivity) that were encountered, the number and percentage of locations where a species was collected, the drainage basin in which it was collected, and the percentage of streams and/or ponds in which it was collected are shown, for most species, in Tables 3, 4, 5, and 6, respectively.

Color is imparted by two types of cells, those that contain pigments and those that reflect or refract light. Changes in coloration due to pigmentation are controlled by the nervous system. These changes may be rapid, taking only a few seconds, or slow, requiring hours. Cells that reflect light off the body of a fish helps it blend into the background by reflecting the predominant colors of the environment. The iridescent sheen (e.g., purples, pinks, greens, blues, or yellows), which may vary with species, is caused by light that is refracted when a fish is viewed at different angles.

Color, in conjunction with certain anatomical features, can be a useful characteristic to identify fish. However, color is a highly variable characteristic that not only varies between species but also differs among individuals of the same species. Affecting the color of a fish are a number of factors such as gender, life stage, and habitat. Males, for example, are generally brighter than females and during the spawning season their colors may become even more intense. The young of many freshwater species often have dark lateral bands or blotches on their sides that usually fade as the fish becomes older. Fish living in turbid or darkly stained waters or over dark substrates may be darker than fish living under brighter conditions such as in clear water or over light colored substrates.

More information on the fishes that were collected during the Stream and Pond Survey can be found in a variety of publications that include Bigelow and Schroeder 1953; Perlmutter 1961; Thomson et al. 1971; Scarola 1973; Scott and Crossman 1973; McClane 1974; Everhart 1976; Wang and Kernehan 1979; Lee et al. 1980; Boschung, Jr. et al. 1983; Smith 1985; Robin and Ray 1986; Page and Burr 1991; Jenkins and Burkhead 1993; Whitworth 1996; Fuller et al. 1999; Steiner 2000; Hartel et al. 2002; Werner 2004; and Langdon et al. 2006; Jacobs and O'Donnell 2009. The common and scientific names used in this publication are in accord with those proposed by the American Fisheries Society Special Publication 29, Sixth Edition, Common and Scientific Names of Fishes from the United States, Canada, and Mexico (Nelson et al. 2004).
Information can also be found on the internet:

Froese, R. and D. Pauly. Editors. 2009. FishBase.
World Wide Web electronic publication.
www.fishbase.org, version (10/2009).

Fuller, Pam. 2009.
USGS (United States Geological Survey)
NAS (Nonindigenous Aquatic species) Program
http://nas.er.usgs.gov

Lampreys
Family Petromyzontidae

Lampreys are primitive fish that are distributed worldwide in temperate freshwater and marine environments. Lampreys are characterized by a circular, sucker-like mouth that lacks true jaws, the absence of paired fins, several pore-like gill openings, and a scaleless eel-like body having a long dorsal fin. Two species were collected: a small non-parasitic freshwater species and a larger anadromous species that is parasitic.

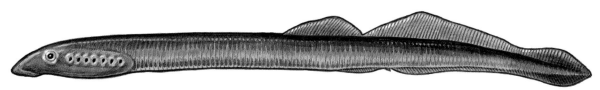

American brook lamprey
Lampetra appendix

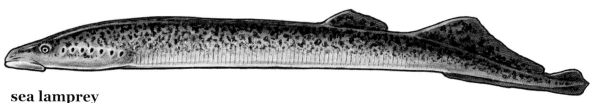

sea lamprey
Petromyzon marinus

American brook lamprey

American brook lamprey
Lampetra appendix (DeKay, 1842)

Distribution: The American brook lamprey is a native freshwater species that was collected from six stream locations in the northeastern part of the state. Most were collected from sandy and/or silty substrates. In North America, the American brook lamprey occurs along Atlantic Slope drainages from New Hampshire to Virginia and in the St. Lawrence and Mississippi River basins.

Identification: This small olivaceous fish, whose color becomes yellowish ventrally, reaches lengths of approximately 8 inches (203 mm). A sucker-like mouth that lacks true jaws and several pore-like gill openings distinguishes this species from the American eel, which has true or hinged jaws and a single set of gill openings. Unlike the parasitic sea lamprey, the teeth of adult brook lamprey are less prominent and fewer in number.

Remarks: Upon hatching, young brook lampreys, known as ammocoetes, drift downstream and burrow into areas with soft substrates where they remain for several years feeding on microscopic plant and animal life. At this stage of life the mouth or oral disk lacks teeth and is surrounded by a fleshy hood, which is lost after it metamorphoses into an adult. Adults are not parasitic and do not feed after reaching maturity, as their intestines have degenerated, and die soon after building a nest and spawning. The Rhode Island Natural Heritage Program has listed the American brook lamprey as State Threatened because of the likelihood of it becoming State Endangered in the future if current trends in habitat loss and other detrimental factors remain unchecked. In Massachusetts and Connecticut it is listed as threatened and endangered, respectively.

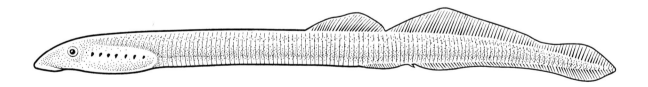

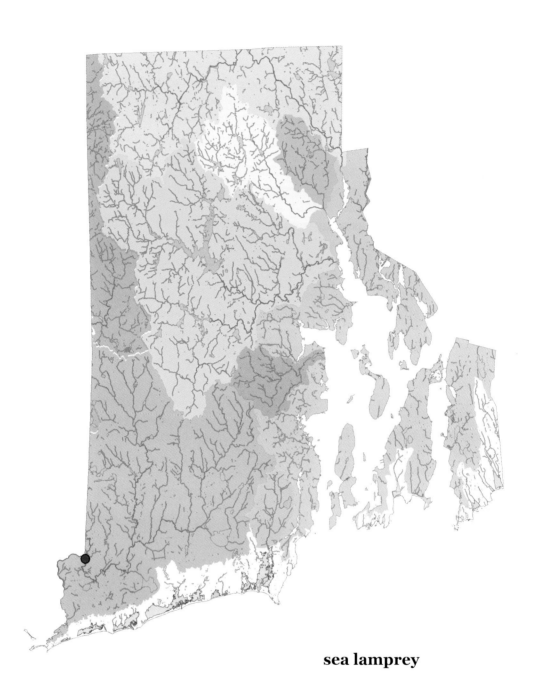

sea lamprey

sea lamprey
Petromyzon marinus Linnaeus, 1758

Distribution: Young sea lampreys, approximately 12 inches (305 mm) in length, are occasionally found attached to adult American shad migrating into the Pawcatuck River to spawn. Sea lampreys were never encountered elsewhere in the state. Spawning populations of this anadromous species, however, are found nearby in Connecticut and Massachusetts. Sea lampreys are distributed along the Atlantic Coast from Nova Scotia south to Florida and in the drainages of the St. Lawrence River and the Great Lakes, as well as the Atlantic coast of Europe. The sea lamprey is not native to the Great Lakes. Prior to the construction of the Welland Canal that was built to bypass Niagara Falls, sea lampreys had no access to the Great Lakes as Niagara Falls acted as a natural barrier.

Identification: Adult sea lampreys, reaching lengths of approximately 48 inches (122 cm), are olive to orange in color with dark mottling, which becomes whitish ventrally. Young sea lampreys are generally grayish dorsally with dark mottling and whitish below. Unlike the American brook lamprey, the sea lamprey is parasitic and has many sharp conical teeth that it uses to attach itself to a host.

Remarks: After attaching itself to its host, the sea lamprey rasps a hole through the skin with teeth located on its tongue and feeds on the bodily fluids. Like the American brook lamprey, adults die soon after spawning.

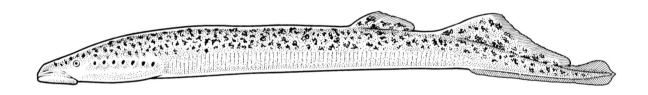

Freshwater eels
Family Anguillidae

This family, which consists of only a single genus, *Anguilla*, is widely distributed in temperate and tropical areas of the world.   The American eel (*Anguilla rostrata*) is the only species found in North America. Like the European eel (*Anguilla anguilla*), the American eel lives in fresh and brackish water, and spawns in the Sargasso Sea. The American eel is characterized by a single set of paired fins, the pectoral fins, a snake-like body having dorsal and anal fins that are continuous with the caudal fin, and a small gill slit that is located in front of the pectoral fins. Although not apparent, tiny scales are embedded in a slime-coated skin. Unlike the lampreys, another family having a snake-like body, freshwater eels have true or hinged jaws.

American eel
Anguilla rostrata

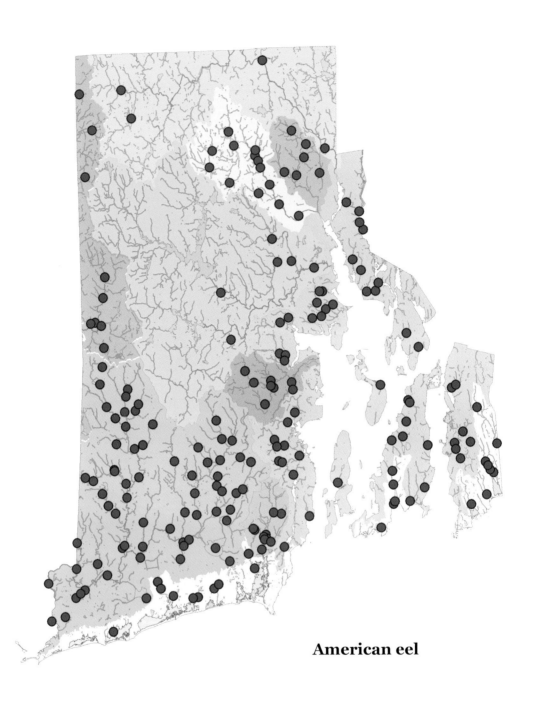

American eel

American eel
Anguilla rostrata (Lesueur, 1817)

Distribution: The American eel, a native catadromous species, was the most widely distributed species collected, occurring in more than 52 percent of the locations sampled, in all ten drainages, and in both lotic and lentic environments. Dams appear to have significantly limited their distribution in the Blackstone, Ten Mile, and Pawtuxet River drainages. Numerous surveys in Wilson Reservoir and Echo Lake show that a few American eels have successfully migrated into the upper reaches of the Blackstone. This native fish is distributed along Atlantic and Gulf Coast drainages from Labrador to South America, the islands of the Caribbean, and the Great Lakes and St. Lawrence River drainages.

Identification: American eels ranging in length from approximately 2.5 to 36 inches (64 – 914 mm) were collected. When fully mature, eels may reach lengths of approximately 60 inches (152 cm), with males typically smaller than females. The color of adults is variable, ranging from olive-brown to almost black. As with most fish, its dorsal surface is darker than its ventral surface. The conger eel (*Conger oceanicus*) is a marine species that looks very similar to the American eel. A characteristic that easily distinguishes the two species is the insertion or origin of the dorsal fin. The origin of the dorsal fin on the conger is over or slightly behind the tips of the pectoral fins whereas on the American eel the origin is well behind the pectorals. Unlike lampreys, American eels have true jaws, a single gill opening on each side of the head, and pectoral fins.

Remarks: Upon reaching maturity, an adult eel migrates downstream to the ocean where it makes its way to the Sargasso Sea to spawn (females may lay as many as two million eggs). After hatching the young eels drift northward, undergoing a series of developmental stages. In the spring the young eels enter estuaries where they may remain or continue with their upstream migration. The young eels may take several years (7 to 20) to mature before migrating back to sea. Female eels grow larger and mature later than males. Eels are nocturnal, bottom-dwelling predators that feed on a variety of invertebrates and fish as well as on dead animal matter. They are an important prey species for such sport fish as bluefish and striped bass and for many bird species. Overfishing and habitat degradation (e.g., dams and water quality) are attributed to the decline in its abundance. A number of measures such as eel ramps and harvest regulations are in place in an attempt to rebuild stocks.

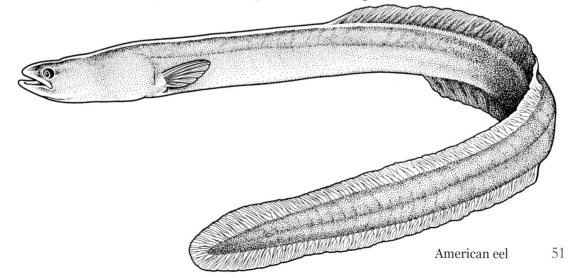

Anchovies
Family Engraulidae

Anchovies are small herring-like fish that are characterized by a snout that extends beyond a large subterminal mouth and a large eye. They are distributed worldwide in temperate and tropical environments. Typically occurring in inshore waters, many can tolerate a wide range of salinities. Thirty species occur in North America.

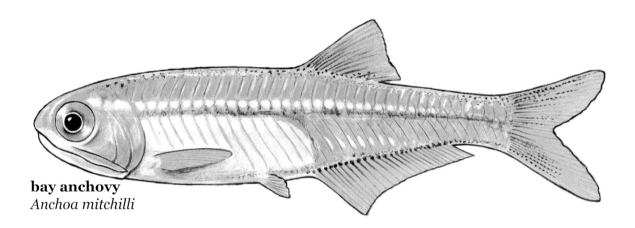

bay anchovy
Anchoa mitchilli

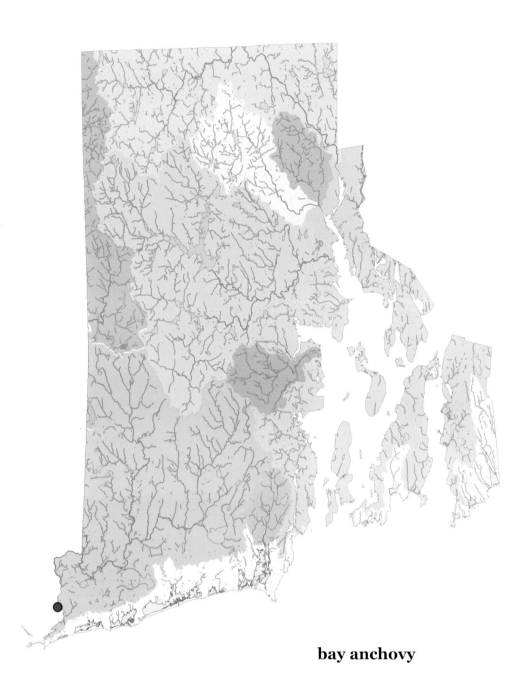

bay anchovy

bay anchovy
Anchoa mitchilli (Valenciennes, 1848)

Distribution: The bay anchovy is a native, coastal marine species that is collected infrequently in the brackish water of the lower Pawcatuck River. This fish has also been collected elsewhere in the coastal waters of Rhode Island (Satchwill 2003). The bay anchovy ranges along the Atlantic Coast from Maine to Florida, preferring sandy beaches and the mouths of rivers. Bay anchovies are year-round inshore residents that undergo seasonal offshore migrations during cold weather.

Identification: This small fish, averaging approximately 3 inches (76 mm) in length, has a translucent, silvery white or pinkish body with a narrow silvery longitudinal band along both sides. It is characterized by a snout that extends beyond a large subterminal mouth, a maxillary that extends well behind a large eye, and by a single dorsal fin. Typical of this species is the location of the anal and dorsal fins. The origin of the anal fin is almost directly beneath the origin of the dorsal fin.

Remarks: Bay anchovies are of little commercial importance but are, however, an important link in the food chain. Anchovies feed on a variety of zooplankton and in turn are fed upon by larger predatory fish such as weakfish and striped bass or by fish-eating birds.

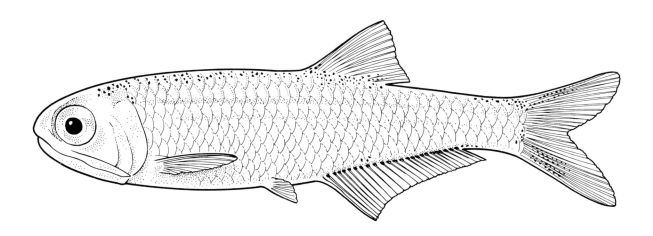

Herrings
Family Clupeidae

Clupeids are widely distributed throughout the world. Six species, among 33 species that are found in North America, were collected. The bodies of most clupeids are deep and laterally compressed with sharp saw-like scales located ventrally along the midline, hence the name "saw-bellies." All in this family are characterized by a single dorsal fin. Species from the genus *Alosa* are anadromous and are well known for their seasonal spring migrations. The scales of anadromous species tend to shed easily and can frequently be seen coating the bottom of a stream during the spring spawning run. When handled, the scales are easily sloughed off. Many herring are filter-feeders, straining the water for zooplankton, fish eggs, fish larvae, etc.

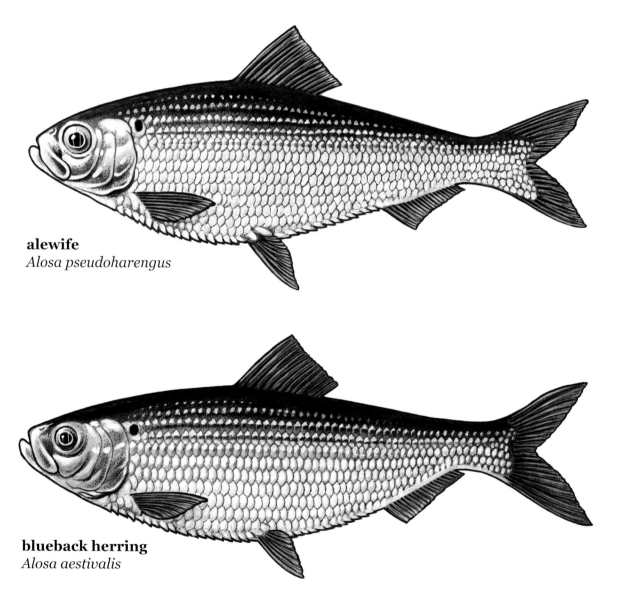

alewife
Alosa pseudoharengus

blueback herring
Alosa aestivalis

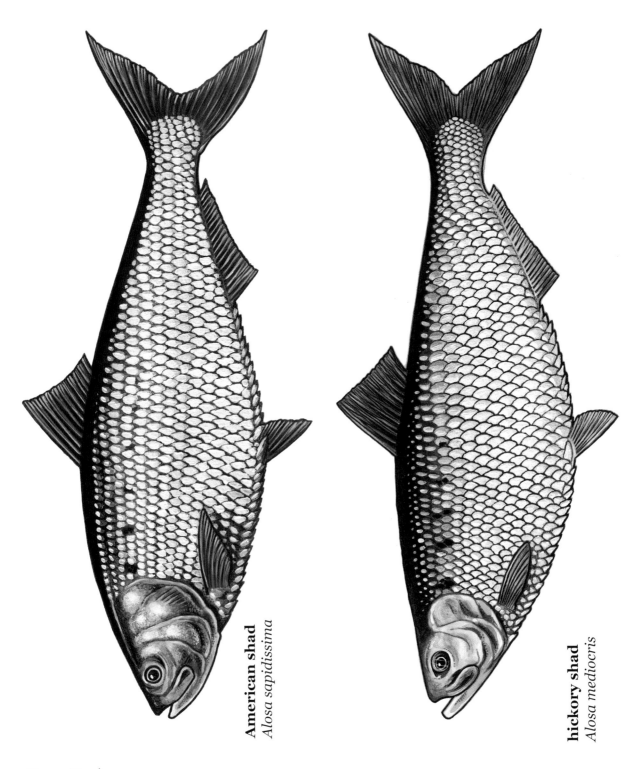

American shad
Alosa sapidissima

hickory shad
Alosa mediocris

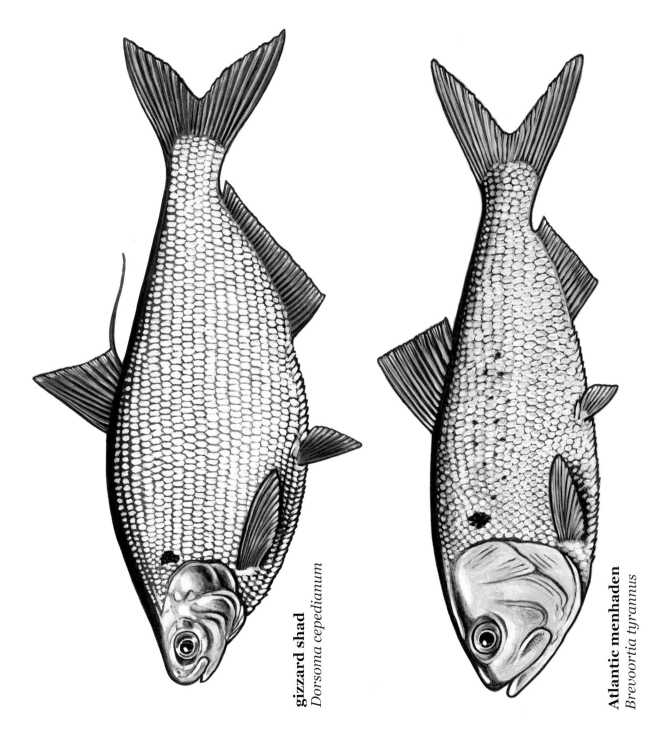

gizzard shad
Dorsoma cepedianum

Atlantic menhaden
Brevoortia tyrannus

Herrings   59

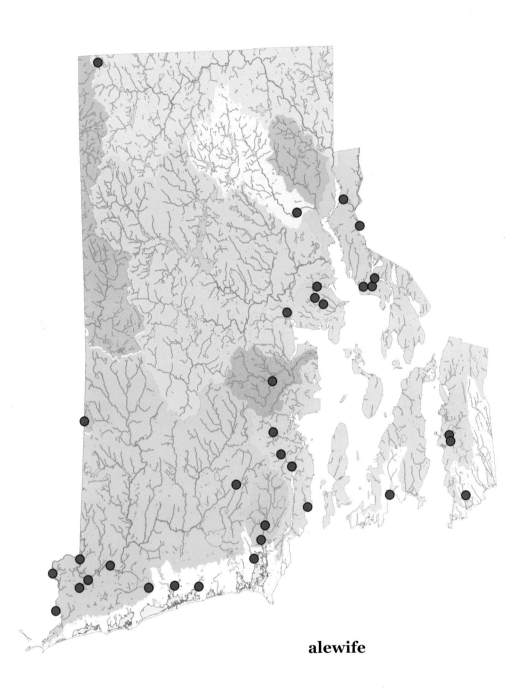

alewife

alewife
Alosa pseudoharengus (Wilson, 1811)

Distribution: The alewife is a native, anadromous species that was collected in the streams and ponds of several watersheds. Landlocked populations were also collected in Hundred Acre Pond, Beach Pond, and Wallum Lake. The landlocked population found in Hundred Acre Pond was first reported in the 1950s by Saila and Horten (1957). The populations in Beach Pond and Wallum Lake were established in the 1960s when they were stocked to provide a forage base for a program to produce trophy-sized salmonids (Lapin 1992). Although not collected during the present survey, alewives were collected in earlier surveys of Stafford Pond (Edwards and Olszewski 1990). In North America alewives range along the Atlantic Coast from Labrador to South Carolina, and into the St. Lawrence River and Great Lakes.

Identification: Landlocked and sea-run alewives as long as 8.8 inches (224 mm) and 12 inches (305 mm), respectively, were collected. Landlocked alewives tend to be smaller in size than sea-run alewives and males tend to be smaller than females. Alewives are characterized by dark blue-gray backs and silvery sides, which become whitish lower on the body. Faint longitudinal stripes may sometimes be noted along the sides. Iridescent sheens of blue, yellow, or green can also be observed on fresh specimens. Alewives look very similar to blueback herring, which often makes it difficult to distinguish between the two as they are about the same size. However, in comparison to the blueback herring the diameter of the eye of the alewife is greater than the length of its snout (see below). The peritoneum of the alewife is grayish and pale in contrast to the black or sooty colored peritoneum of the blueback herring.

The length of the maxillary and the shape of the cheek distinguish the alewife from the American shad. The maxillary of the alewife extends to a point below the middle of the eye, whereas the maxillary of the American shad extends to a point below the rear of the eye. The cheeks of alewives are as wide as they are deep, but in the case of the American shad, the cheek is deeper than it is wide.

Remarks: Because of their similarity in appearance, alewives and blueback herring are collectively referred to as river herring. A decline in the population of these commercially important fish has, at the present time, resulted in the season being closed to the harvest of these species in Rhode Island's marine and freshwaters.

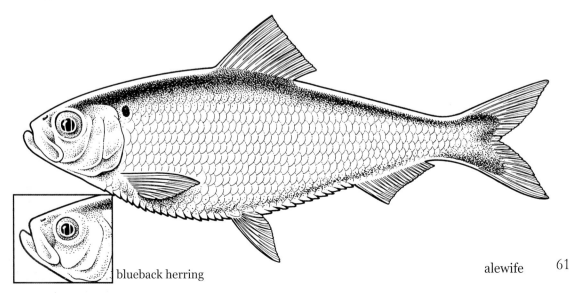

blueback herring

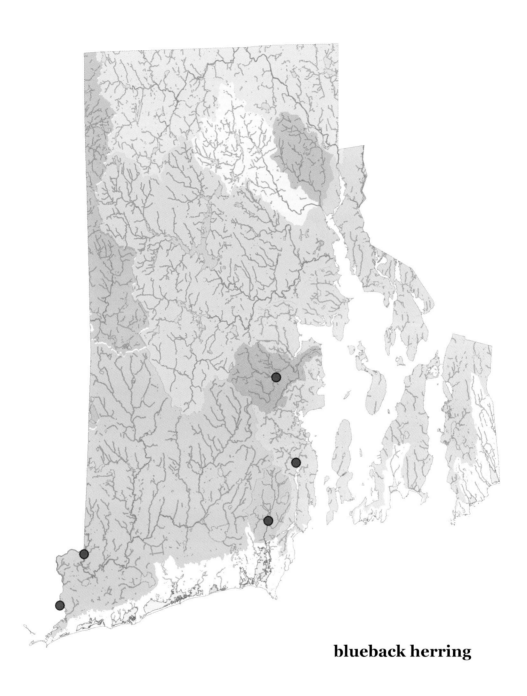

blueback herring

blueback herring
Alosa aestivalis (Mitchill, 1814)

Distribution: This native, anadromous species was found in a few streams and ponds in the Pawcatuck, Saugatucket, and Hunt Rivers. Both adult and young-of-the-year blueback herring were collected. Blueback herring range along Atlantic Coast drainages from Maine to Florida.

Identification: Blueback herring as long as 11 inches (279 mm) were collected. Blueback herring have dark blue-green backs with silvery sides, which become whitish below. A greenish sheen or iridescence can sometimes be noted in fresh specimens. Blueback herring look very similar to alewives but unlike the alewife, the diameter of the eye of the blueback herring is usually smaller than the length of the snout (see below) and the peritoneum is black or sooty in color.

Two characteristics, the length of the maxillary and the shape of the cheek, distinguish this species from the American shad. The maxillary of the blueback herring extends to a point below the middle of the eye, whereas the maxillary of the American shad extends to a point below the rear of the eye. The cheeks of the blueback herring are as wide as they are deep as opposed to the American shad where the cheeks are deeper than they are wide.

Remarks: Because of their similarity in appearance, blueback herring and alewives are collectively referred to as river herring. A decline in the population of these commercially important fish has, at the present time, resulted in the season being closed to the harvest of these species in Rhode Island's marine and freshwaters.

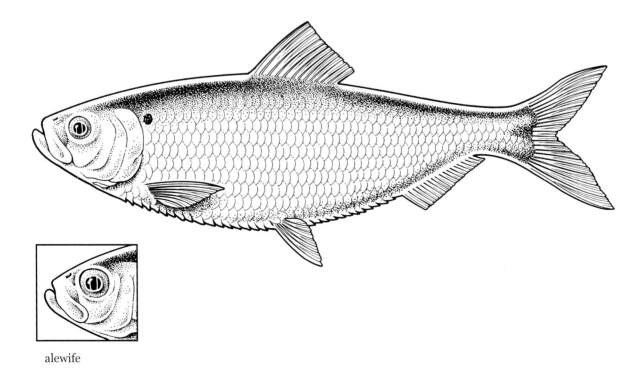

alewife

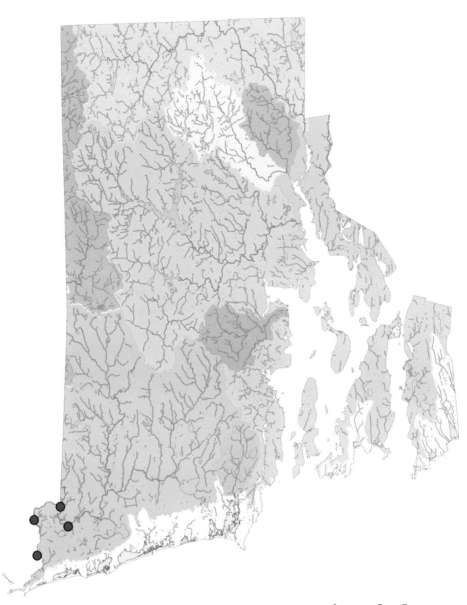

American shad

American shad
Alosa sapidissima (Wilson, 1811)

Distribution: The American shad is a native, anadromous species that was only collected in the lower Pawcatuck River. However, American shad have been collected elsewhere in the coastal waters of Rhode Island (Satchwill 2003). American shad occur along Atlantic Coast drainages from Labrador south to Florida and west into the St. Lawrence River, over-wintering offshore in the Middle Atlantic region of the US. It has also been introduced to the Pacific Coast of the United States.

Identification: Adults as long as 20 inches (508 mm) and young-of-the-year were collected. This species is the largest member of the herring family and can reach lengths of approximately 30 inches (762 mm). The back of the American shad is dark blue and its sides are silvery, becoming whitish below. An iridescent sheen can also be noted with hints of purple, pink, green, yellow, and blue. The mouth of this filter-feeder is terminal.

The shape of the cheek and the length of the maxillary, distinguish this species from river herring. The cheek of the American shad is deeper than it is wide, in contrast to river herring, where the cheeks are as wide as they are deep. The maxillary of the American shad is longer than river herring, extending to a point below the rear edge of the eye.

Remarks: The harvest of American shad is strictly regulated because of a decline in the population of this commercially important species. At the present time, the season is closed on the taking of this species in Rhode Island's marine and freshwaters.

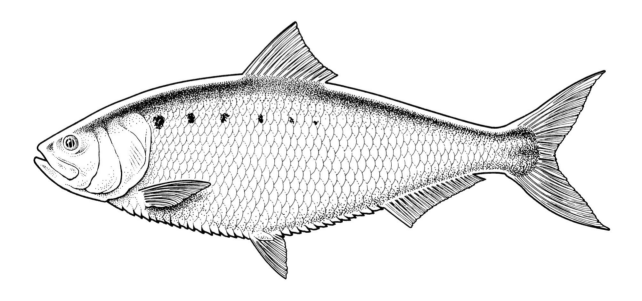

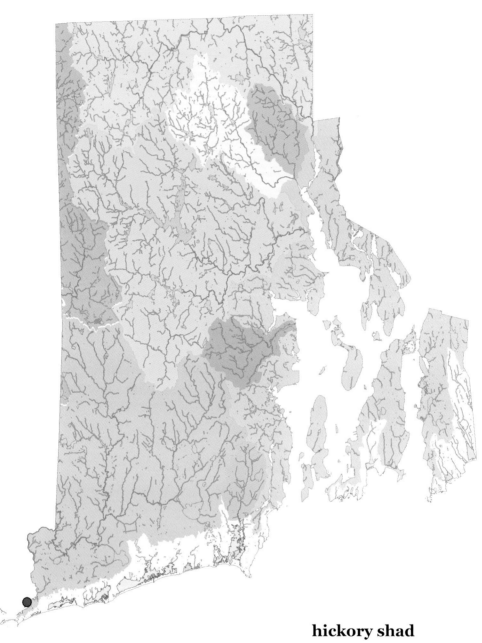

hickory shad

hickory shad

hickory shad
Alosa mediocris (Mitchill, 1814)

Distribution: This anadromous species was collected from a single location near the mouth of the Pawcatuck River. Hickory shad have also been collected elsewhere in the coastal waters of RI (Satchwill 2003). They are often caught by anglers in the state's coastal waters during the summer. Hickory shad range along the Atlantic Coast from Florida to New Brunswick. Spawning generally takes place in coastal rivers in the southern part of its range, from Maryland to Florida.

Identification: Hickory shad are smaller than American shad, reaching lengths of approximately 24 inches (610 mm), but are larger than river herring. Specimens collected during this survey averaged 16 inches (406 mm) in length. Its upper body is bluish and its sides are silvery, becoming whitish below. An iridescent sheen can also be observed on fresh specimens. Faint, dusky longitudinal stripes may also be observed along its sides. The lower jaw, projecting distinctly beyond the snout, is characteristic of this species.

Remarks: At the present time there is no regulation on the harvest of this species. This planktivorous fish feeds on a variety of other organisms such as fish, squid, and crustaceans.

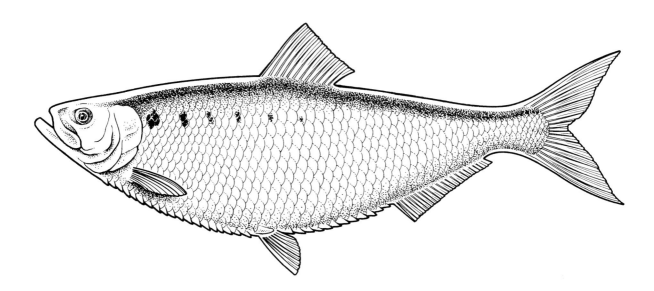

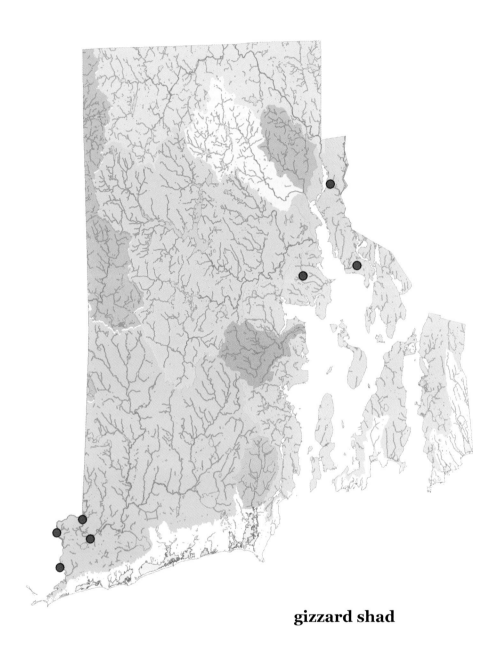

gizzard shad

gizzard shad
Dorsoma cepedianum (Lesueur, 1818)

Distribution: The gizzard shad is a native species that was collected from seven locations, four of which were in the fresh and brackish waters of the lower Pawcatuck River. Young gizzard shad were collected for the first time during the present survey in Brickyard Pond. Gizzard shad occur in Atlantic Coast drainages from Massachusetts south to Florida, and in inland waters from the St. Lawrence River and Great Lakes south to the Gulf of Mexico. Data suggest that the range of gizzard shad is expanding in the northeast (Hartel et al. 2002).

Identification: This fish can reach lengths of approximately 20 inches (508 mm). Its upper body is bluish and its sides are silvery, becoming whitish below. An iridescent sheen can be noted on fresh specimens. These shad are characterized by a blunt rounded snout, a subterminal mouth that does not extend beyond the eye, and by a long filamentous ray (the last ray) in the dorsal fin.

Remarks: The gizzard shad, a filter-feeding omnivore that feeds along the bottom on small plants and animals, is of little commercial value.

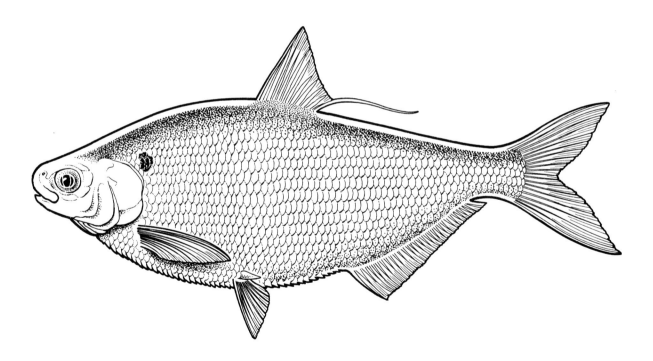

Atlantic menhaden

Atlantic menhaden
Brevoortia tyrannus (Latrobe, 1802)

Distribution: The Atlantic menhaden is a marine species that was collected in the lower Pawcatuck River and in Mill Creek. Each year large numbers of juvenile menhaden, approximately 1 to 5 inches (25 - 127 mm) long, are collected in the brackish waters of the lower Pawcatuck River during the fall. Adults, approximately 11 inches (279 mm) long, were collected near the mouth of the Pawcatuck in more saline waters. Large numbers of Atlantic menhaden have been collected elsewhere in the coastal waters of Rhode Island (Satchwill 2003). Atlantic menhaden are distributed along the Atlantic Coast from Nova Scotia to Florida. This seasonal migrant is common in the state's coastal waters during the summer, moving offshore or south during the winter months.

Identification: Atlantic menhaden can reach lengths of approximately 18 inches (457 mm). These fish have a characteristically large scaleless head, in comparison to other clupeids, that is nearly one third of its standard body length. The Atlantic menhaden is bluish-green dorsally with silvery sides that become whitish below. The body has an overall brassy luster.

Remarks: Atlantic menhaden, often referred to as pogies, feed by filtering plankton from the water with their gill rakers. They are important prey for a wide variety of predators such as striped bass and bluefish. The Atlantic menhaden is an important commercial species that is used as bait to catch lobsters and sport fish such as striped bass. It is also a major source of omega-3 fatty acids used by the health industry to help fight heart disease.

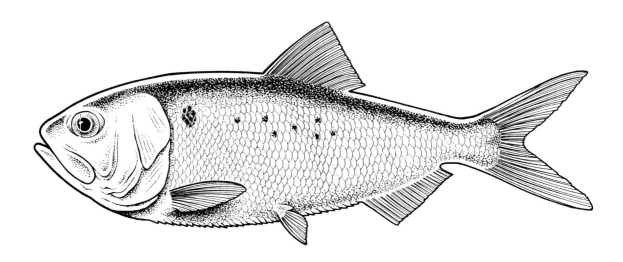

Carps and Minnows
Family Cyprinidae

This large family, consisting of approximately 2,000 species, is distributed worldwide in the freshwaters of temperate and tropical regions. Of the more than 300 species occurring in North America, eight were collected during the survey. Members of this family occur in a variety of body shapes and sizes and are characterized by a single dorsal fin and a mouth that lacks teeth. Teeth, however, are found in the throat on pharyngeal bones located behind the gill arches. Several species also possess barbels near the mouth.

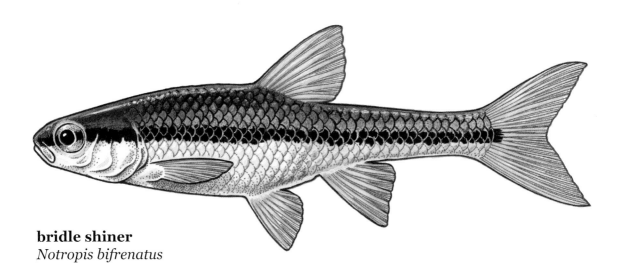

bridle shiner
Notropis bifrenatus

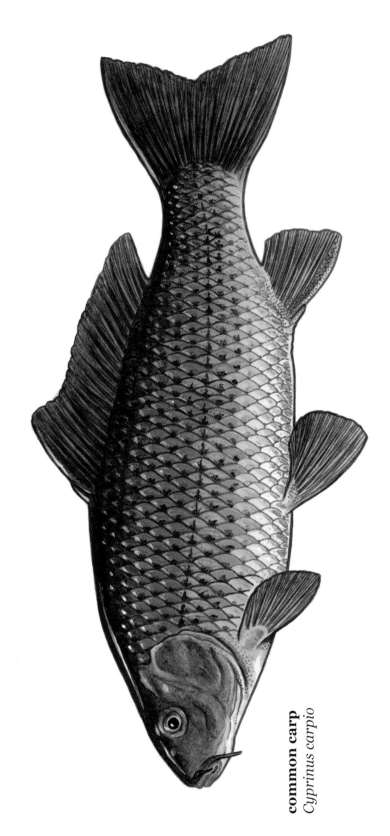

common carp
Cyprinus carpio

Carps and Minnows

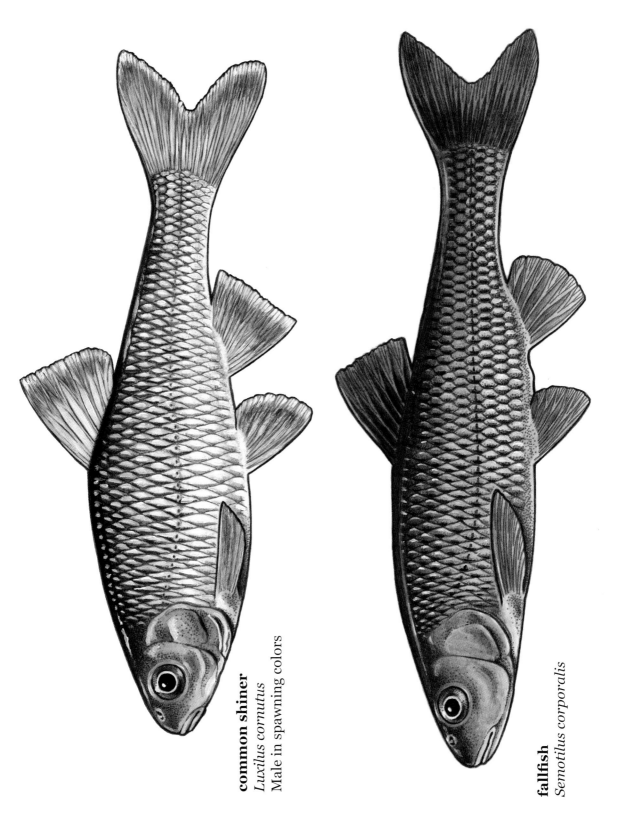

common shiner
Luxilus cornutus
Male in spawning colors

fallfish
Semotilus corporalis

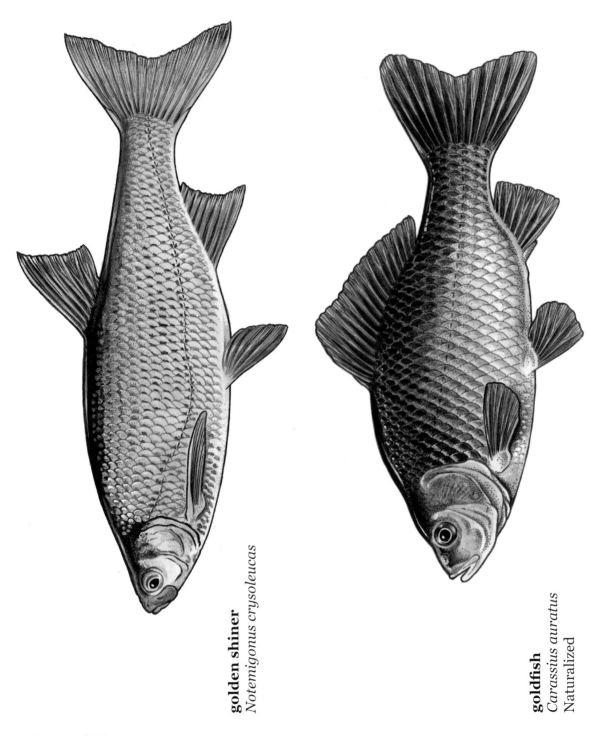

golden shiner
Notemigonus crysoleucas

goldfish
Carassius auratus
Naturalized

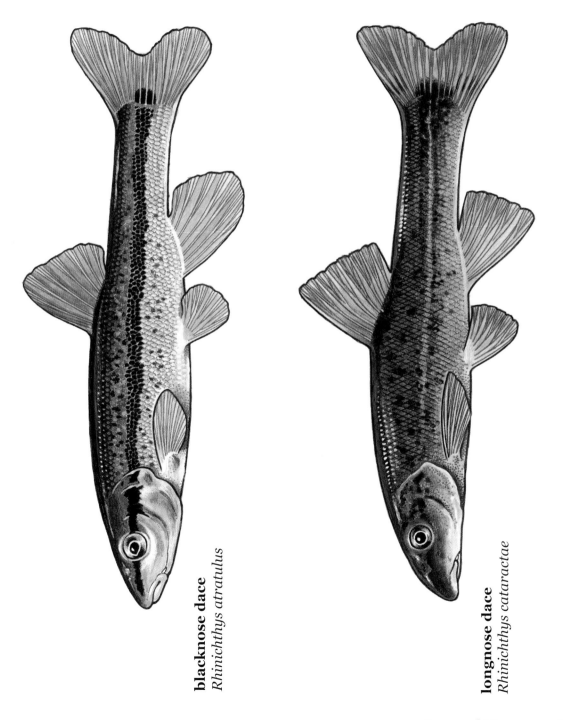

blacknose dace
Rhinichthys atratulus

longnose dace
Rhinichthys cataractae

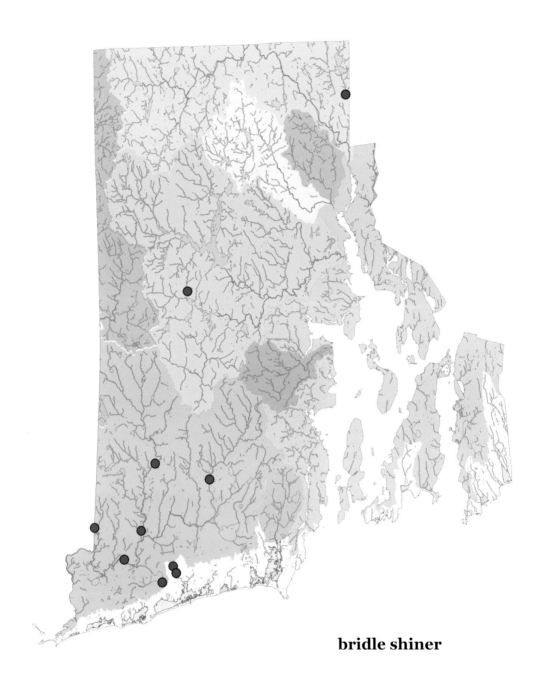

bridle shiner

bridle shiner
Notropis bifrenatus (Cope, 1867)

Distribution: The bridle shiner is a small, native, freshwater species that was collected primarily in the vegetated areas of streams and ponds in the Blackstone, Pawcatuck, Pawtuxet, and coastal Atlantic drainages. Rarely were more than three individuals collected at one time. Bridle shiners are found in Lake Ontario and St. Lawrence drainages and from southern Maine south to Virginia and the Carolinas.

Identification: The bridle shiner, seldom reaching more than 2.5 inches (64 mm) in length, is pale yellow or straw-colored with a distinctive dark mid-lateral band that extends from the tip of the snout to the end of the caudal peduncle. It lacks a complete lateral line and barbels.

Remarks: This little shiner feeds on small aquatic invertebrates, especially insect larvae, copepods, and cladocerans. Data collected in other states suggest that bridle shiners are declining in the Northeast (Whittier et al. 1997).

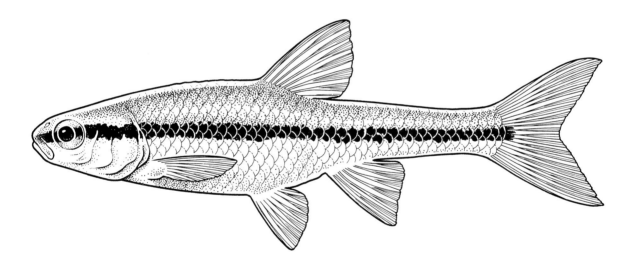

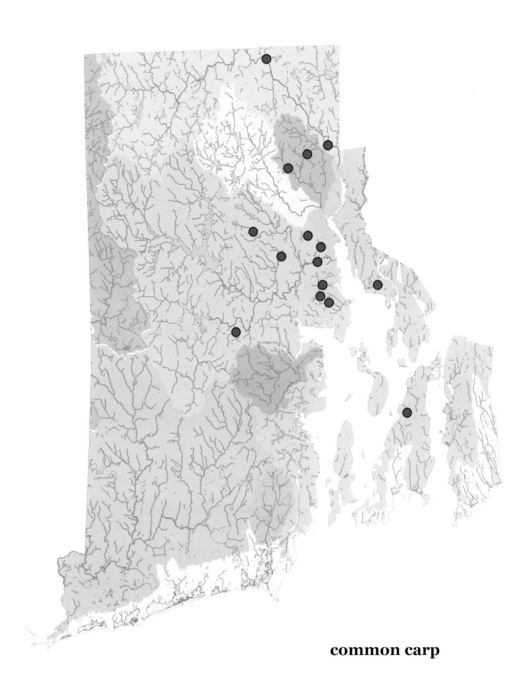

common carp

common carp
Cyprinus carpio Linnaeus, 1758

Distribution: Native to Europe and Asia, this exotic freshwater species was first intro-duced to Rhode Island in 1880 and was collected, for the most part, in urban streams and ponds. The common carp has become widespread and is now found throughout the world.

Identification: The common carp is the largest member of this family found in Rhode Island. Fish longer than 24 inches (610 mm) were routinely collected.   The sport fishing record in Rhode Island is 32.5 pounds (3.5 kg). This robust fish is bronze or olive-brown in color that fades to white or yellowish ventrally. Koi, a colorful ornamental strain of the com-mon carp that was developed in Japan, were collected in Melville and Meshanticut Ponds. Unlike other fish in this family, except for the goldfish, carp have long dorsal fins containing 14 or more rays and a single serrated spine located on the anterior edges of the dorsal and anal fins. Two pairs of barbels located on the upper jaw also distinguish this species from other individuals in the family. Carp typically have a uniform number (35-39) of scales along the lateral line, but on some individuals may be scattered or absent. These fish are often referred to as "mirror" or "leather" carp.

Remarks: Carp are omnivores that feed by rooting in the sediments, sucking plant mate-rial, aquatic invertebrates, fish eggs and larvae, etc. into their mouths and expelling unwant-ed matter into the water. This type of feeding behavior is detrimental to the environment because it increases the turbidity of the water and reduces the number of eggs and larvae of desirable native species. Carp are tolerant of many environmental conditions and can sur-vive in unfavorable conditions that many other species cannot.

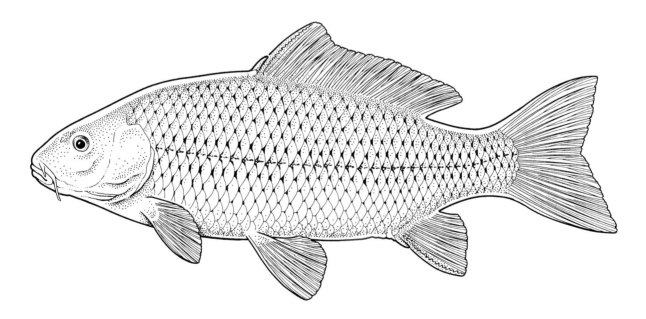

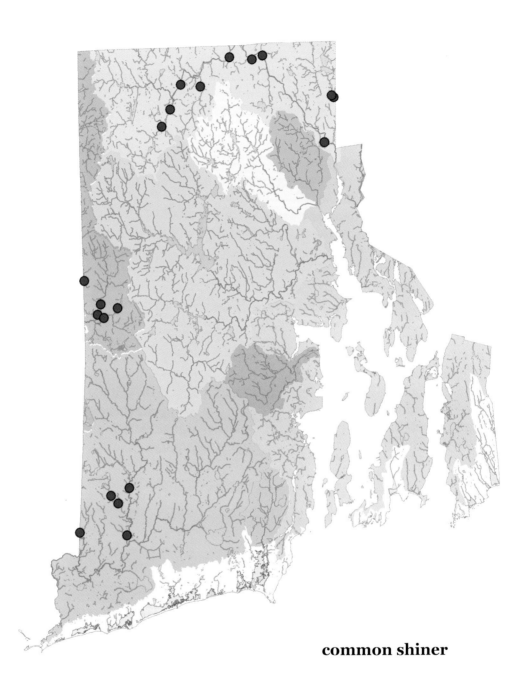

common shiner

common shiner
Luxilus cornutus (Mitchill, 1817)

Distribution: The common shiner is a native, freshwater species that was found in several watersheds located in the northern and western areas of the state. It was collected exclusively in streams, its preferred habitat. This species occurs along Atlantic Coast drainages from Nova Scotia to Virginia and west to Wyoming and Saskatchewan.

Identification: Common shiners as long as 7 inches (178 mm) were collected. This shiner is olive or a gun-metal blue dorsally with silvery sides, becoming white ventrally. The fins of mature fish are pale with reddish margins. During the breeding season the red margins become more brilliant in males. Small nuptial tubercles are found on the heads and the dorsal surface of breeding males. The young of common shiners and fallfish are silvery and very similar in appearance. However, unlike the fallfish, common shiners have no barbels. The relationship between the height of the anterior most lateral scales and their width is also useful to distinguish this species from the fallfish. The anterior most scales of the common shiner are distinctly more than twice as high as they are wide, whereas the scales of the fallfish tend to be more rounded.

Remarks: The diet of the common shiner includes a variety of organisms and some plant material, but consists mainly of terrestrial and aquatic invertebrates such as worms and small fishes. It is a popular bait fish in some areas.

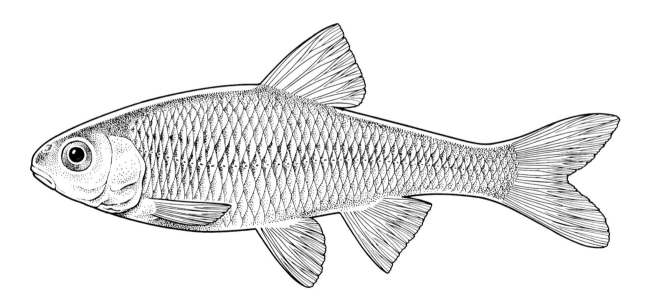

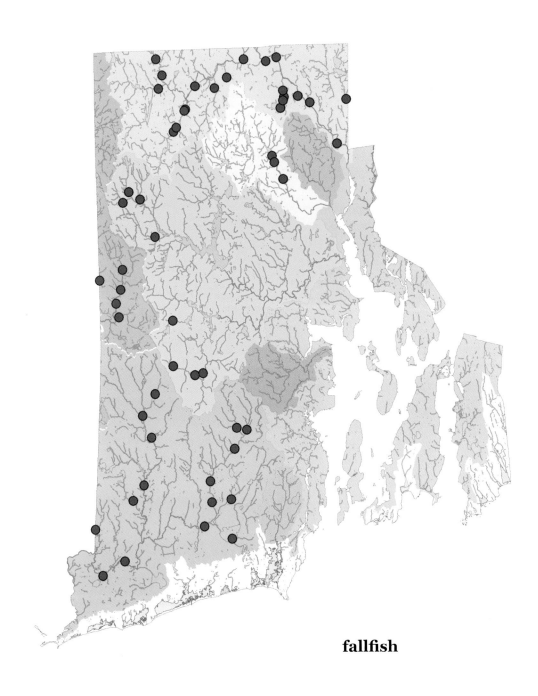

fallfish

fallfish
Semotilus corporalis (Mitchill, 1817)

Distribution: This native freshwater minnow was collected for the most part in lotic environments, its preferred habitat. Among the five drainages in which it occurred, this stream species was more widely distributed in the Pawcatuck and Blackstone watersheds. The fallfish is found in Quebec, Ontario, New Brunswick, and Atlantic Coast drainages south to Virginia.

Identification: The fallfish is the largest of the native freshwater minnows occurring in Rhode Island. Although lengths exceeding 17 inches (432 mm) are sometimes attained, the largest fish encountered was 13 inches (330 mm) in length. Fallfish can vary in coloration. Older fish tend to be olive-brown or bronze in color, which becomes lighter in shade lower on the body. Young fish are silvery with a bluish metallic luster and have a dark mid-lateral band along their sides that fades as it matures. A small triangular barbel is sometimes hidden in the posterior end of the maxillary groove on either side of the jaw. On rare occasions one or more barbels may be absent. The relationship between the height of the most anterior lateral scales and their width is useful to distinguish this species from the common shiner. The anterior most scales on the fallfish tend to be more rounded as opposed to the common shiner, where the scales are distinctly more than twice as high as they are wide.

Remarks: Fallfish feed on a variety of aquatic insect larvae, terrestrial insects, crustaceans, and fish.

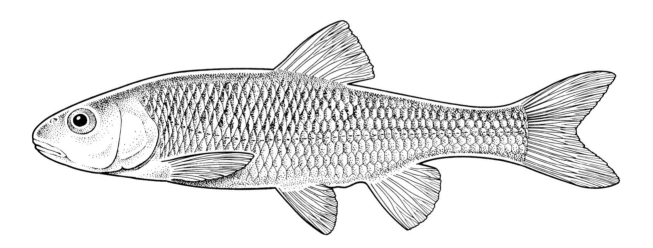

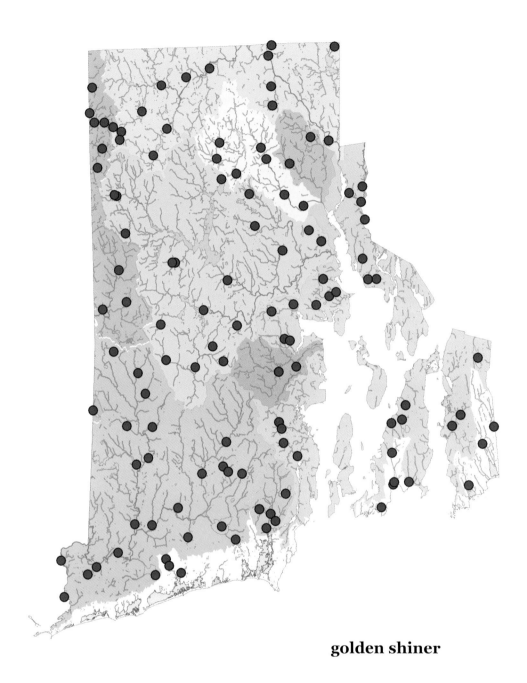

golden shiner

golden shiner
Notemigonus crysoleucas (Mitchill, 1814)

Distribution: This native, freshwater species was the seventh most widely distributed species collected, occurring in more than 30 percent of the locations sampled, all ten drainages, and in more than 70 percent of the ponds sampled. This species occurs along Atlantic Coast drainages from Nova Scotia to Florida and west to Texas and Saskatchewan.

Identification: Golden shiners of all sizes were collected; the largest was 11.5 inches (292 mm) long. Adults are deep-bodied (i.e., the body is distinctly compressed, laterally) and golden in color. Juveniles are silvery and have a dark lateral band that extends from the gill covers to the caudal fin. This dark band fades with age. Characteristic of this species is a lateral line that dips noticeably toward the pelvic fins and a scaleless keel located between the anus and pelvic fins.

Remarks: The golden shiner is commonly sold as bait in Rhode Island. It feeds on a variety of small organisms including aquatic and terrestrial insects, molluscs, and algae and is, in turn, an important forage species for such game fish as largemouth bass and northern pike.

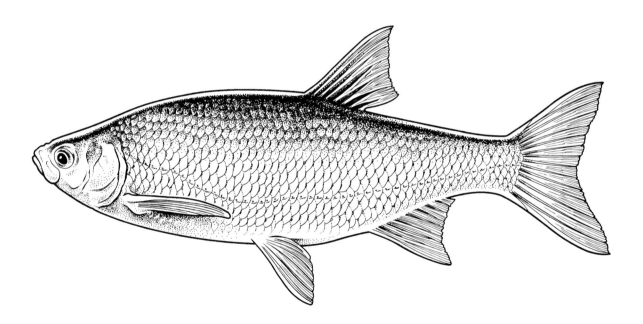

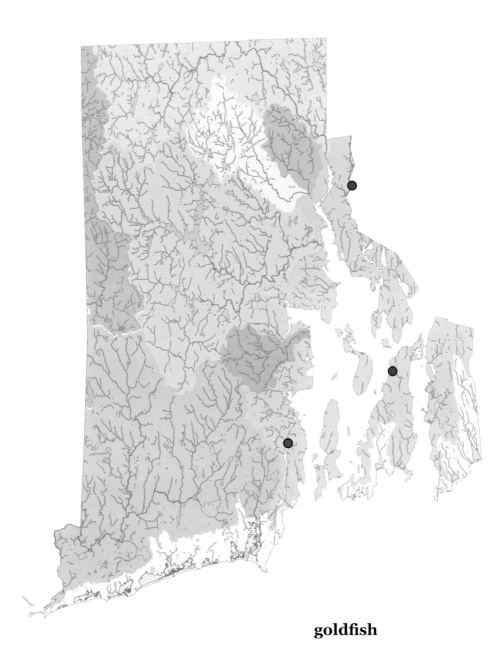

goldfish

goldfish
Carassius auratus (Linnaeus, 1758)

Distribution: This exotic and sometimes colorful fish is native to Asia, but is now widely distributed throughout the world. It is a very popular aquarium and water garden fish that was first cultured in China. Goldfish were collected from three locations: Turner Reservoir, the Mattatuxet River below Gilbert Stuart Road, and Barker Brook. Their presences are the results of illegal introductions. The olive drab color of the goldfish caught in Barker Brook suggests that it belonged to a naturalized population. The goldfish collected in Turner Reservoir and the Mattatuxet River may have been recent introductions as they were still very colorful and had never been collected in previous surveys (Guthrie and Stolgitis 1977; Army Corps of Engineers 2001).

Identification: Goldfish as long as 5 inches (127 mm) were collected. Adults range in length from approximately 5 to 16 inches (127 – 406 mm). Goldfish raised for the aquarium trade are orange, white, black, or any combination of these colors. Wild or naturalized populations gradually revert back to their natural olive drab coloration. Unlike other fish in this family, except for the carp, goldfish have long dorsal fins containing 14 or more rays and a single serrated spine located on the anterior edges of the dorsal and anal fins. The absence of barbels on the upper jaw distinguishes the goldfish from carp and koi.

Remarks: Goldfish are omnivorous, feeding on a wide variety of plants and animals. Their feeding behavior may result in increases in turbidity and decreases in aquatic vegetation. It is illegal to use goldfish as bait in Rhode Island.

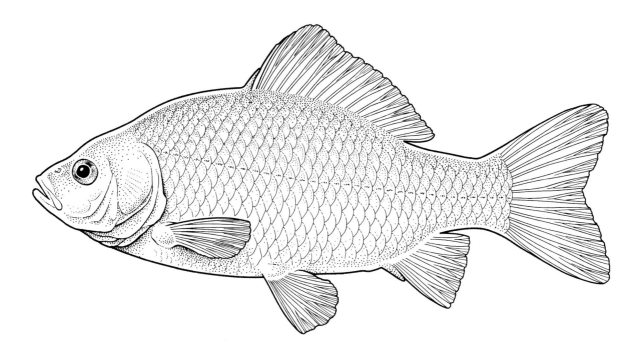

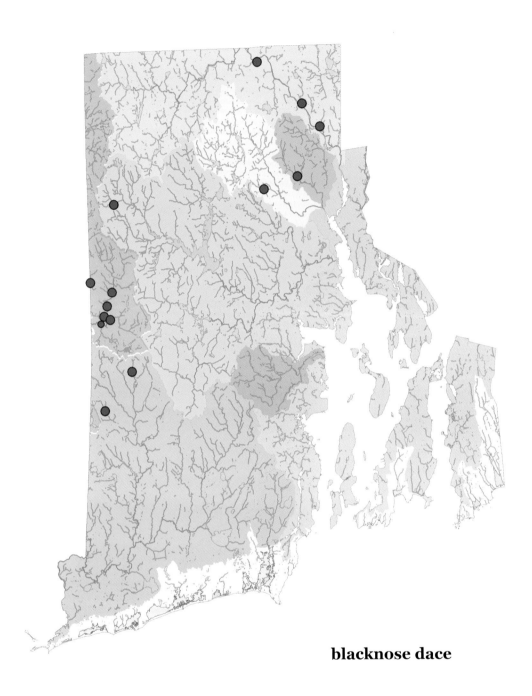

blacknose dace

blacknose dace
Rhinichthys atratulus (Hermann, 1804)

Distribution: The blacknose dace is a native, freshwater species whose distribution was limited to a few widely scattered streams, its preferred habitat. The blacknose dace occurs in southern Canada from Nova Scotia west to Manitoba southward to the Great Lakes and the Mississippi River Basin to Georgia, Alabama, and South Carolina.

Identification: The dorsal surface of this small fish, seldom reaching lengths of more than 3.5 inches (89 mm), is generally a dark olive-brown color. A dark longitudinal stripe that extends from the tip of its snout to the caudal fin, separates the darker dorsal surface from a pale whitish coloration below. Both the blacknose dace and the longnose dace are characterized by a barbel located on each side of the jaw at the posterior end of the maxillary and by a small band of tissue (the frenum) that connects the upper lip with the snout. The location of its eyes in relation to its mouth and the length of its snout distinguish the blacknose dace from the longnose dace (see below). For the blacknose dace, the bottom edge of the eye is about level with the uppermost edge of its mouth. The mouth is subterminal and located slightly behind the snout. The length of the snout, measured from the tip of the snout to the forward edge of the lower jaw, is less than the width of its eye.

Remarks: This species feeds on a variety of organisms, particularly aquatic insect larvae.

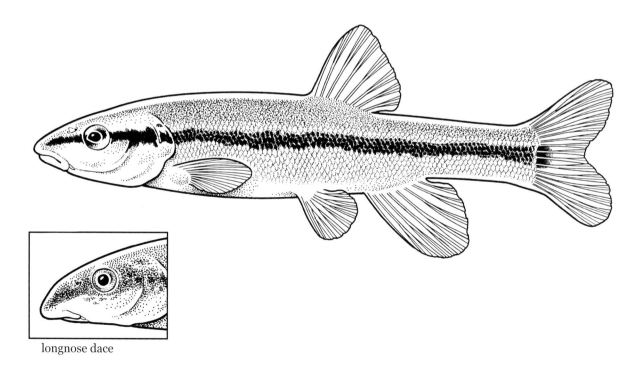

longnose dace

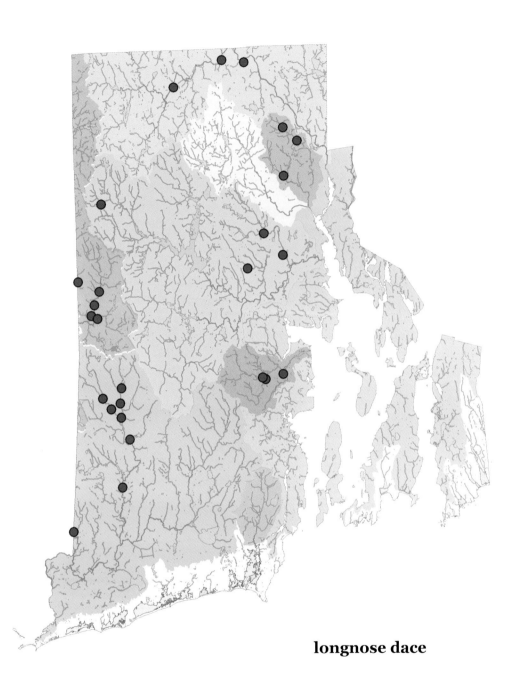

longnose dace

longnose dace
Rhinichthys cataractae (Valenciennes, 1842)

Distribution: The longnose dace is a native, freshwater species with a somewhat limited distribution. It was found primarily in the gravelly riffles of streams, its preferred habitat. Longnose dace are present throughout much of North America from Canada south through the Rocky and Appalachian Mountains.

Identification: This relatively small species seldom reaches more than 5 inches (127 mm) in length. The back and sides are dark brown with some mottling, whereas the ventral surface is lighter in color. A dark lateral band that is commonly found on younger fish tends to fade with maturity and may be lacking entirely on older fish. Both the longnose dace and the blacknose dace are characterized by a barbel located on each side of the jaw at the posterior end of the maxillary and by a small band of tissue (the frenum) that connects the upper lip with the snout. The location of its eyes in relation to its mouth and the length of the snout distinguish the longnose dace from the blacknose dace (see below). For the longnose dace, the bottom edge of the eye is usually well above the uppermost edge of the mouth. The mouth is inferior and located well behind the snout. The length of the snout, measured form the tip of the snout to the forward most edge of the lower jaw, is about equal to the width of its eye.

Remarks: This benthic species feeds on a variety of aquatic invertebrates.

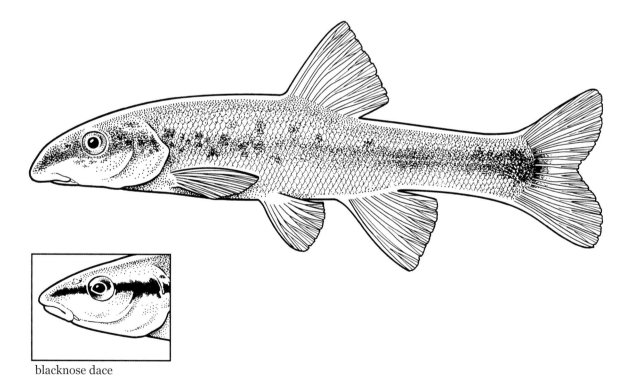

blacknose dace

Suckers
Family Catostomidae

This family is principally found in North America (72 species) but also occurs in Siberia and China. Mouths are subterminal or inferior with characteristically large fleshy lips that are useful for identification. Two species are found in Rhode Island.

white sucker
Catostomus commersoni

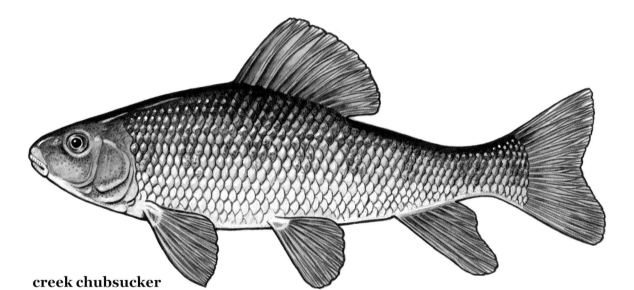

creek chubsucker
Erimyzon oblongus

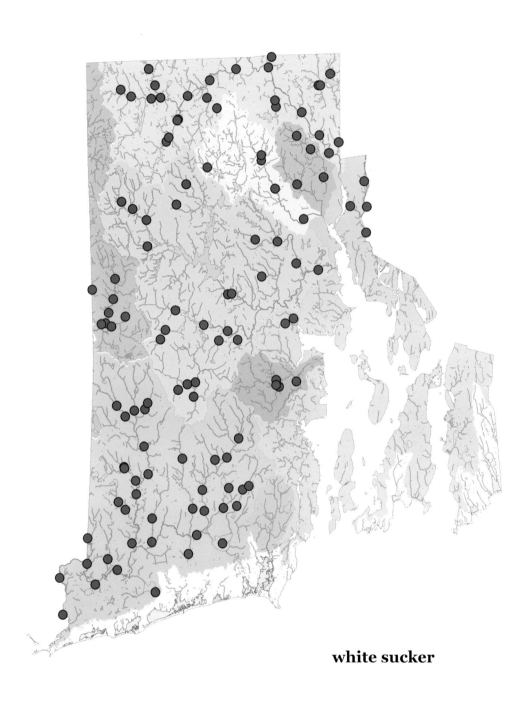

white sucker

white sucker
Catostomus commersoni (Lacepede, 1803)

Distribution: This native freshwater species was the tenth most widely distributed species collected. It occurred in more than 30 percent of the localities sampled, eight drainages, and in a greater proportion of streams than ponds. The white sucker is widely distributed in North America from the Arctic Circle south to New Mexico and Georgia, but is absent from most Pacific coast drainages.

Identification: The white sucker is a torpedo-shaped fish that rarely reaches a length of 20 inches (508 mm). Adults may be brownish or grayish in color dorsally and lighter ventrally. The sides may have a coppery iridescent sheen. Dark blotches are characteristically found on the bodies of juveniles. A complete lateral line and an inferior mouth with fleshy lips covered with papillae distinguish this species from the creek chubsucker.

Remarks: Adult white suckers generally inhabit the quiet waters of streams and ponds but in the spring migrate into the gravelly areas of streams to spawn. The diet of this bottom feeder includes insect larvae, small crustaceans, and worms.

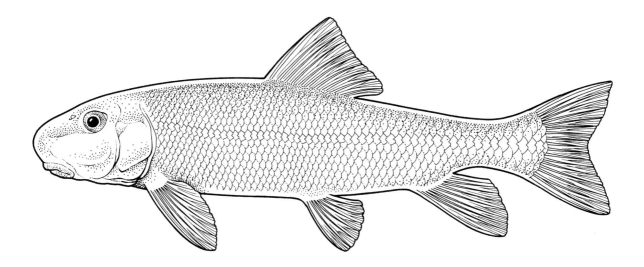

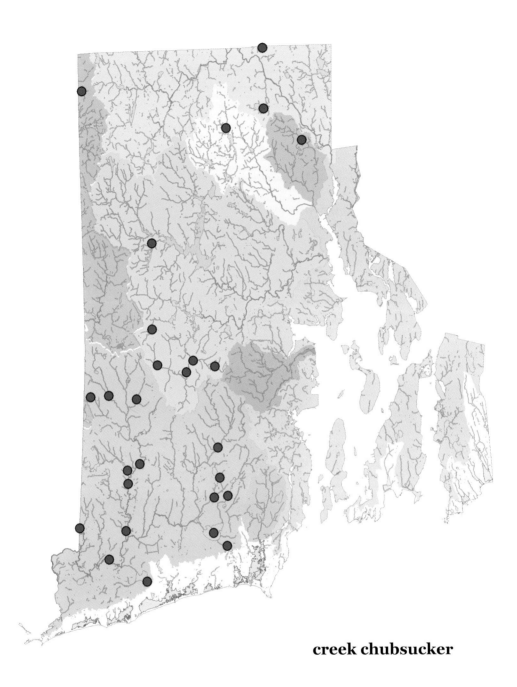

creek chubsucker

creek chubsucker
Erimyzon oblongus (Mitchill, 1814)

Distribution: The creek chubsucker is a native freshwater species that occurred in a greater proportion of ponds than streams. Although not as widely distributed as the white sucker, it was found in six drainages. Creek chubsuckers are found in Atlantic Slope drainages from Maine to Georgia, selected Great Lakes drainages, and in the Mississippi River basin from the southern Great Lakes to the Gulf of Mexico.

Identification: The creek chubsucker is shorter and more robust than the white sucker. The longest specimen collected was 14 inches (356 mm) long. Color varies with age; young creek chubsuckers have a dark dorsal band and black mid-lateral bands. The sides are dusky olive-yellow between the dorsal and lateral band and pale yellow-white below the lateral band. The pectoral, anal, and pelvic fins on medium sized fish may be a ruddy orange. The mid-lateral bands tend to fade as the fish ages, becoming faint vertical bars or blotches on a yellowish body. Unlike the white sucker, the creek chubsucker lacks a lateral line, its subterminal mouth has fleshy pleated lips, and its anal fin is bi-lobed. Tubercles can sometimes be noted on the heads of mature males.

Remarks: Its diet includes aquatic insects, mollusks, small crustaceans, and algae.

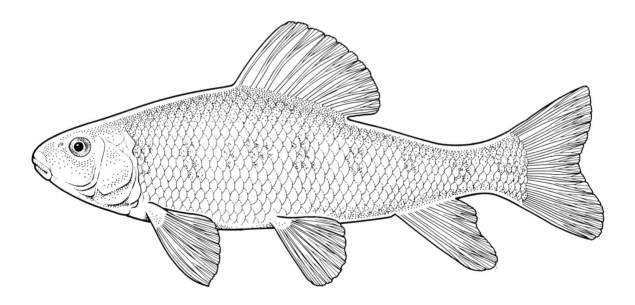

North American Catfishes
Family Ictaluridae

 This family, consisting of 46 species, is indigenous to North America. North American catfishes are characterized by large flattened heads with several pairs of barbels around the mouth. These fish are scaleless, have an adipose fin, and are armed with sharp spines located in the dorsal and pectoral fins. Glands located at the base of the spines release a toxin that can flow along the spines and into a wound, causing a painful sting. The shape of the caudal fins and color of the chin barbels are useful characteristics that distinguish the three species found in Rhode Island.

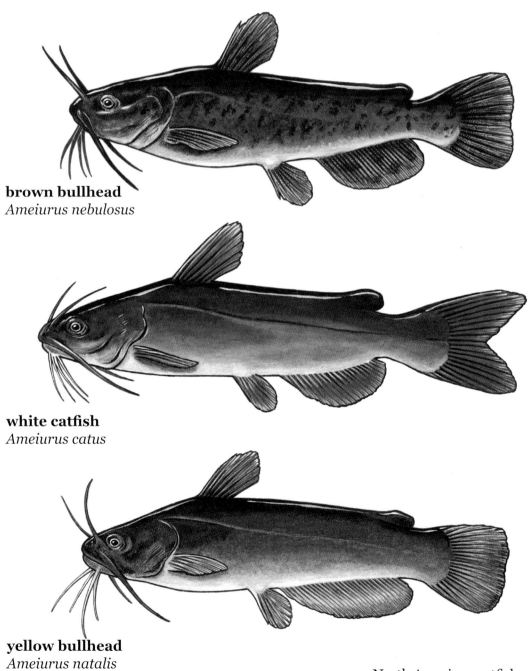

brown bullhead
Ameiurus nebulosus

white catfish
Ameiurus catus

yellow bullhead
Ameiurus natalis

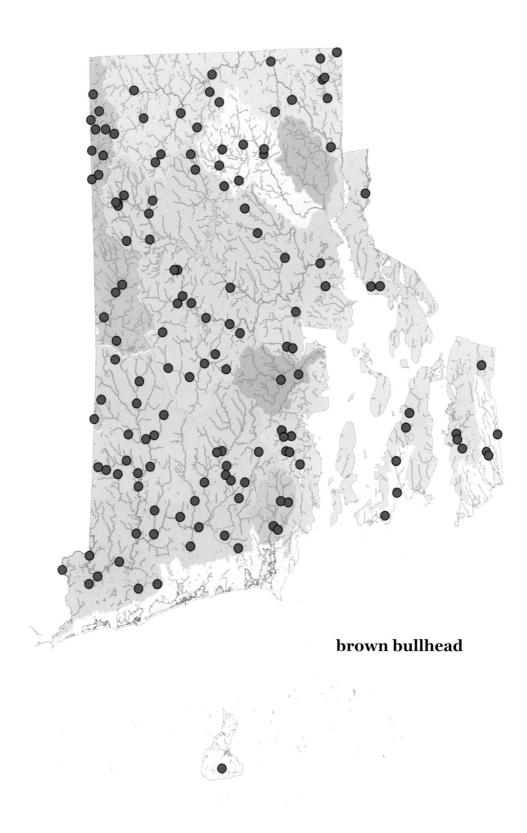

brown bullhead

brown bullhead
Ameiurus nebulosus (Lesueur, 1819)

Distribution: This native, freshwater species was one of the six most widely distributed species collected, occurring in more than 35 percent of the locations sampled and in a greater proportion of ponds than streams. Brown bullheads ranged from approximately 1.25 to 14.75 inches (32 - 375 mm) in length and were generally collected in the vegetated areas of ponds and sluggish streams in all but one watershed. Tolerant of a wide variety of environmental conditions, the brown bullhead is found in Atlantic and Gulf Coast drainages from Nova Scotia to Florida, west to Saskatchewan and Oklahoma.

Identification: Brown bullheads, which may exceed 18 inches (460 mm) in length, are dark olive brown or black dorsally and lighter ventrally. Light and dark mottling may occur along the sides of some individuals. This species is characterized by dark chin barbels and a squared caudal fin that may be slightly indented.

Remarks: The brown bullhead is a benthic omnivore that feeds on a variety of aquatic plants, invertebrates, and fish.

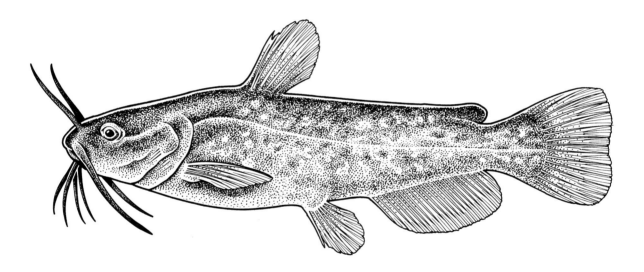

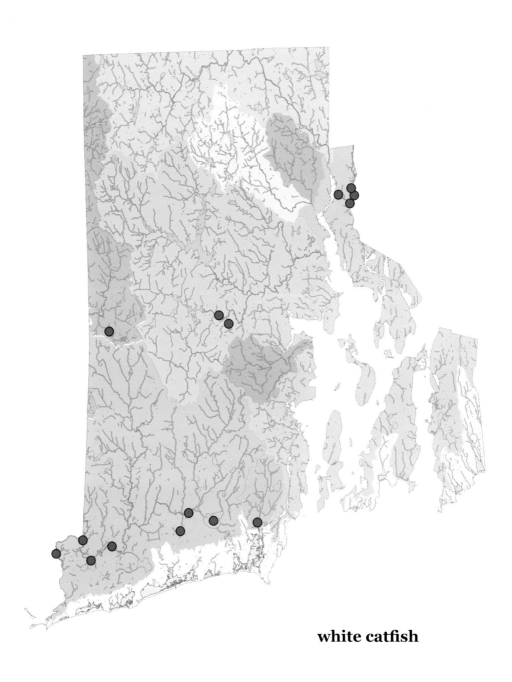

white catfish

white catfish
Ameiurus catus (Linnaeus, 1758)

Distribution: The white catfish is a freshwater species that was introduced into the state in the 1960s. Reproducing populations were documented in a few widely dispersed streams and ponds. The preferred habitat of this species is the vegetated areas of ponds and quiet streams. White catfish are native to Atlantic Coast and Gulf of Mexico drainages from New York to Florida.

Identification: White catfish, which ranged in length from approximately 1.75 to 16 inches (44 – 406 mm), are dark olive brown dorsally, becoming lighter ventrally. This species is characterized by whitish chin barbels and a moderately forked caudal fin with rounded lobes.

Remarks: A 33 inch (838 mm) fish weighing more than 16 pounds (7 kg) was caught in Tiogue Lake, Coventry, in 1994. The white catfish is a benthic omnivore that feeds on a variety of aquatic plants, invertebrates, and fish.

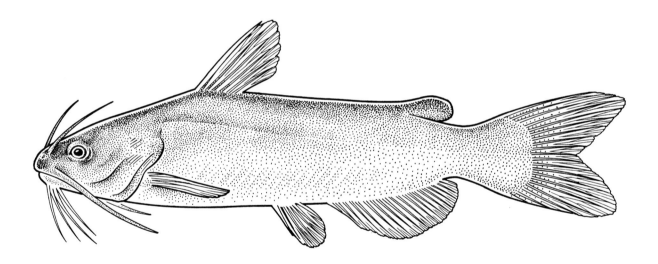

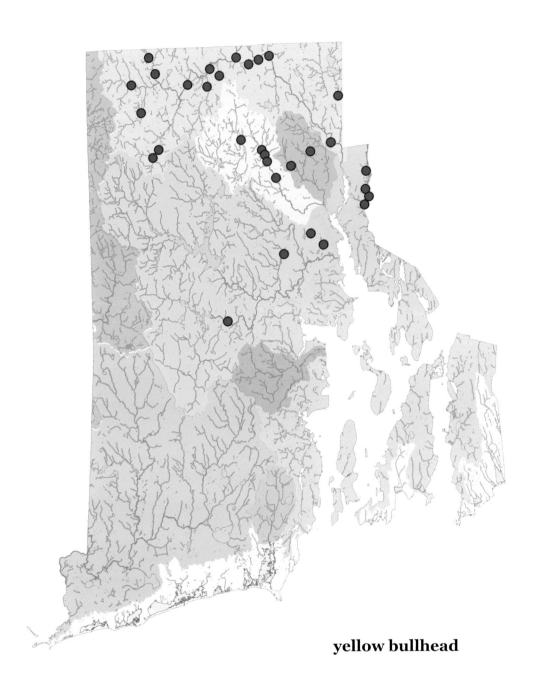

yellow bullhead

yellow bullhead
Ameiurus natalis (Lesueur, 1819)

Distribution: The yellow bullhead is an introduced freshwater species that was collected in the streams and ponds of several watersheds located in the northern half of the state. It is unknown when this species was first introduced in the state. However, it was first collected in a tributary of the Blackstone River in the 1970s (Demaine and Guthrie 1979). The preferred habitat of this bullhead is the vegetated areas of ponds and slow-moving streams. Yellow bullheads are native to eastern North America from New York west to Ontario and North Dakota, and south to New Mexico and Florida. Widely introduced elsewhere, yellow bullheads are also found in Massachusetts and Connecticut waters.

Identification: The yellow bullhead, which may exceed 18 inches (457 mm) in length, is dark olive brown dorsally becoming lighter and somewhat yellowish ventrally. This species is characterized by whitish yellow chin barbels and a rounded caudal fin.

Remarks: The diet of this nocturnal benthic feeder includes plants, aquatic invertebrates, and fish.

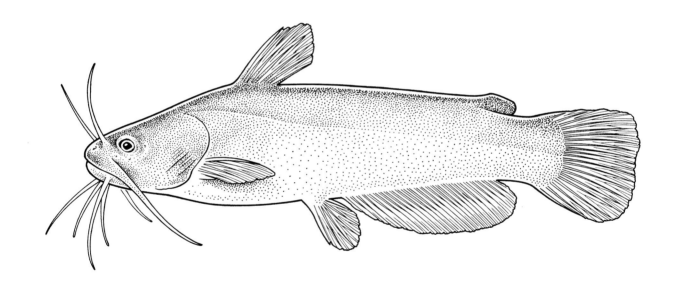

Pikes
Family Esocidae

Members of this family are found in North America, Europe, and Asia. Among the four species that are found in North America, three were collected in Rhode Island. These predatory, freshwater fish are characterized by slender torpedo-shaped bodies, and flattened and elongated, duck-billed shaped snouts. The dorsal and anal fins are located near the rear of the body. Scale patterns on the opercles distinguish the chain and redfin pickerels from the northern pike.

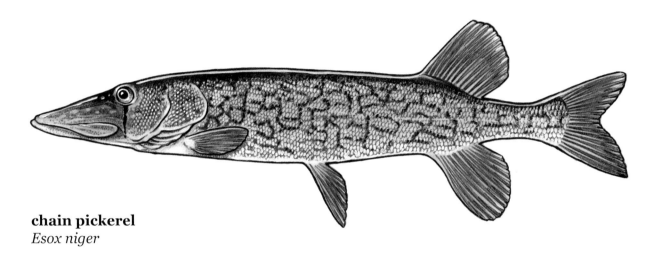

chain pickerel
Esox niger

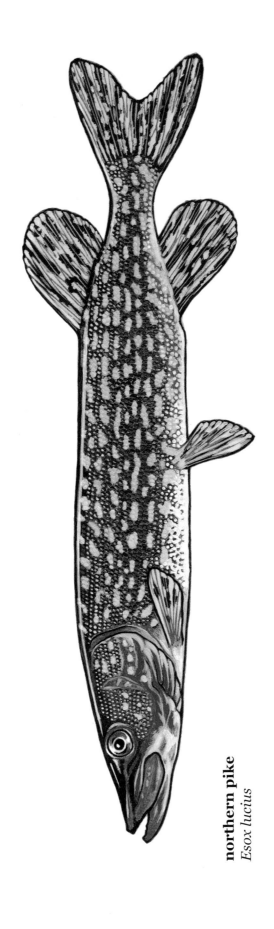

northern pike
Esox lucius

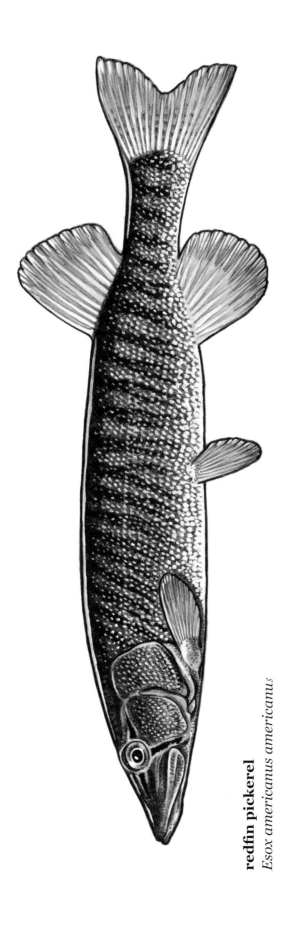

redfin pickerel
Esox americanus americanus

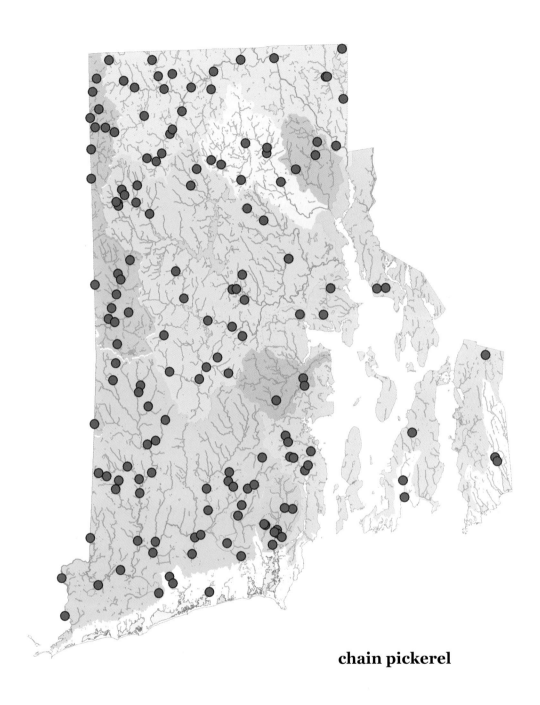

chain pickerel

chain pickerel
Esox niger Lesueur, 1818

Distribution: This native freshwater fish was the fifth most widely distributed species collected, occurring in approximately 40 percent of the locations sampled. Chain pickerel were collected in all ten drainages and from a greater proportion of ponds than streams. In North America the chain pickerel originally occurred in Atlantic and Gulf Coast drainages from Maine to Florida and the lower Mississippi River, but has since become widely introduced elsewhere.

Identification: Chain pickerel specimens ranged in size from approximately 2 to 24 inches (50 – 610 mm). The dorsal surface of a chain pickerel is olive-green or brown. The sides are yellow-green with olive-green or brown chain-like markings and the lower surface tends to be whitish. The young are similar in appearance to the redfin pickerel; that is, the sides have wavy diagonal stripes. Unlike the northern pike, the chain pickerel's opercles are fully scaled. The length of the snout (the distance between the tip of the snout and the anterior edge of the eye) in comparison to the length of the operculum (the distance between the rear edge of the eye and the rear edge of the operculum) easily distinguishes this species from the redfin pickerel (see below). For chain pickerel, snout length is greater than the length of the operculum, whereas for redfin pickerel the snout length is shorter than its operculum length.

Remarks: Chain pickerel are carnivorous, preferring to hide in vegetated areas where they wait to ambush, among other things, unsuspecting fish or frogs.

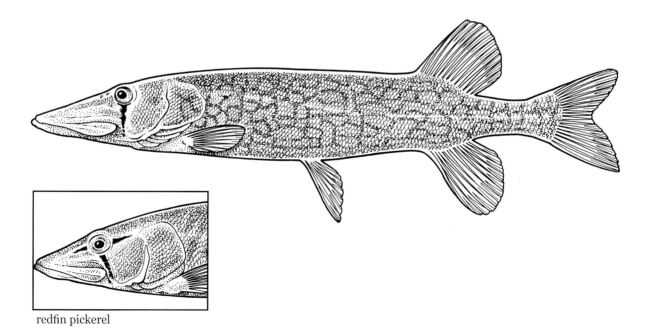

redfin pickerel

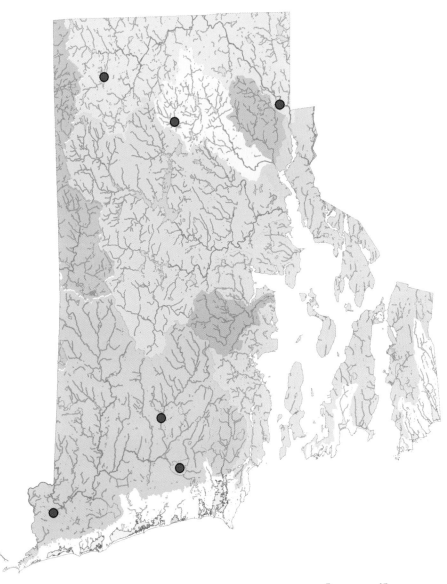

northern pike

northern pike
Esox lucius Linnaeus, 1758

Distribution: Northern pike were introduced in the 1960s and were collected in six locations. Juveniles or naturalized populations were not discovered during the survey. This fish is stocked periodically by the Division in Chapman Pond, Flat River Reservoir (a.k.a. Johnson Pond), Waterman Reservoir, Woonasquatucket Reservoir (a.k.a. Stump Pond), and Worden Pond for a put-and-take fishery. The northern pike is circumpolar in distribution and is found across northern North America, Europe, and Asia. Its southern limit in North America ranges from the Connecticut and Hudson Rivers to Missouri. The northern pike has been widely introduced elsewhere.

Identification: Northern pike may exceed 48 inches (122 cm) in length and are olive-green or brown on the dorsal surface and sides and whitish ventrally. Longitudinal rows of yellowish bean-shaped markings are found along the sides. The young are similar in appearance to the redfin pickerel; that is, the sides have wavy diagonal stripes. The opercles on the northern pike are only scaled on the upper half, a characteristic that distinguishes it from the redfin and chain pickerels, whose opercles are fully scaled.

Remarks: The northern pike, an important game fish, is the largest member of this family found in Rhode Island. A 47.5 inch (121 cm), 35 pound (16 kg) fish is the state sportfishing record. This large carnivore feeds on a wide variety of animals including muskrats, ducks, and fish.

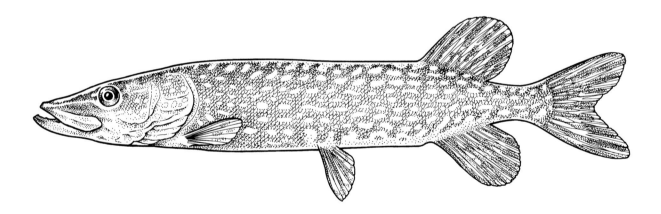

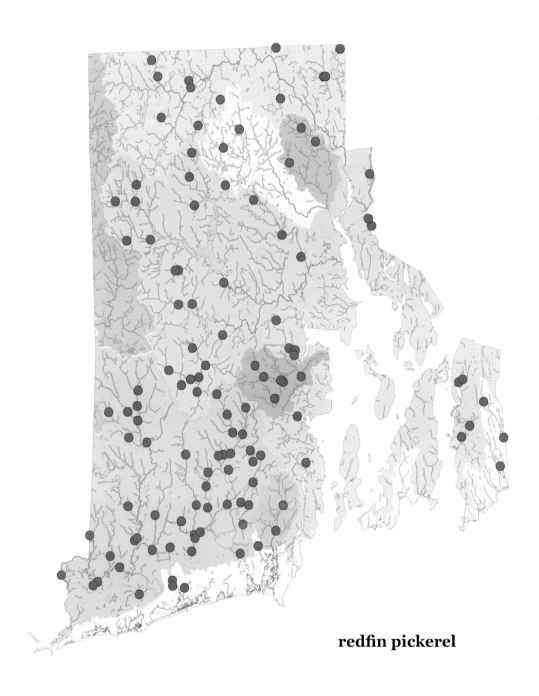

redfin pickerel

redfin pickerel
Esox americanus americanus Gmelin, 1789

Distribution: The redfin pickerel is a native freshwater fish that was the eighth most widely distributed species collected. It occurred in more than 30 percent of the sampling stations. Redfin pickerel were found in a greater proportion of streams than ponds and in most drainages. The redfin pickerel occurs along Atlantic Slope drainages from New Hampshire to Florida. A subspecies, the grass pickerel (*Esox americanus vermiculatus*), is generally found west of the Appalachian Mountains from New York to Texas.

Identification: The redfin pickerel is the smallest member of this family found in Rhode Island. The largest fish collected was approximately 11 inches (279 mm) long. The dorsal surface of a redfin pickerel is olive-green or brown. The sides are marked with alternating olive-green or brown and whitish wavy stripes that slant upwards towards the rear of the fish. The lower surface is whitish. The lower fins of this species are usually reddish or orange in color. Snout length (the distance between the tip of the snout and the anterior edge of the eye) in comparison to the length of the operculum (the distance between the rear edge of the eye and the rear edge of the operculum) distinguishes this species from the chain pickerel. For redfin pickerel the distance between the tip of the snout and the anterior edge of the eye is smaller than the distance between the rear edge of the eye and the edge of the operculum, whereas for chain pickerel its snout length is greater than its operculum length (see below). Fully scaled opercles distinguish this species from the northern pike.

Remarks: Redfin pickerel are carnivorous, preferring to hide in vegetation and woody debris where they wait to ambush their prey.

chain pickerel

Smelts
Family Osmeridae

Smelts are principally found in the northern regions of North America and Asia in both marine and freshwater habitats. Ten species are found in North America. These relatively small, slender fish are characterized by an adipose fin and a large mouth containing numerous well-developed teeth.

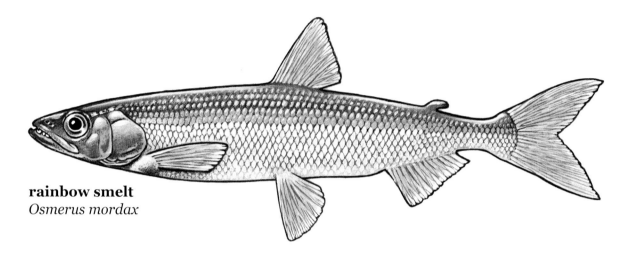

rainbow smelt
Osmerus mordax

rainbow smelt

rainbow smelt
Osmerus mordax (Mitchill, 1814)

Distribution: This native anadromous species was only collected in the lower Pawcatuck River. It has, however, been collected elsewhere in the coastal waters of Rhode Island (Satchwill 2003). In North America, the rainbow smelt is distributed in the inshore waters of the northern Atlantic, Pacific, and Arctic Ocean drainages. It has been introduced elsewhere, including freshwater environments where landlocked populations have been established.

Identification: The rainbow smelt is small and slender, averaging approximately 7 to 9 inches (178 – 229 mm) in length. Smelt as long as 4 inches (100 mm) were collected during the survey. The dorsal surface of the rainbow smelt is pale green or brown. The sides are silvery and the ventral surface is whitish. A purple, pink, or blue iridescence may also be noted along its sides. It is characterized by a large mouth that extends to a point below the middle of the eye, a single dorsal fin, and an adipose fin.

Remarks: Recreational fishing for this tasty little fish generally occurs during the winter ice fishing season in a number of rivers and streams in the northeast. The rainbow smelt is carnivorous and armed with a mouthful of well-developed teeth, including some on its tongue. It feeds on a variety of small invertebrates and fish.

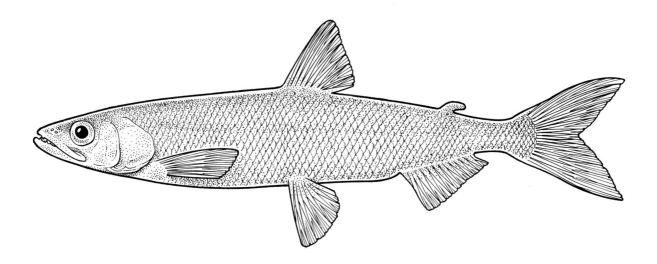

Trouts and Salmons
Family Salmonidae

This family, consisting of both anadromous and freshwater populations, is found in coldwater streams and ponds of North America, Europe, and Asia. Salmonids are characterized by a fleshy adipose fin located between the dorsal and caudal fins, small cycloid scales, and an axillary process located at the base of the pelvic fins. An elongated hooked jaw, referred to as a "kype" may develop on breeding males. Four species, among 38 found in North America, were collected. All four species are considered important game fish.

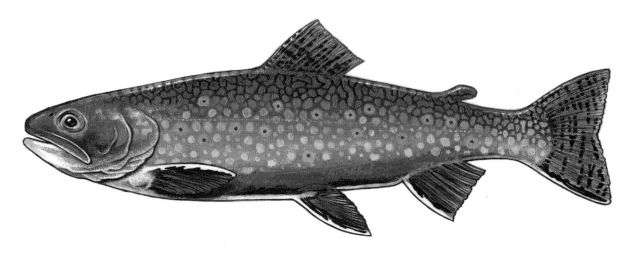

brook trout
Salvelinus fontinalis
Male in spawning colors

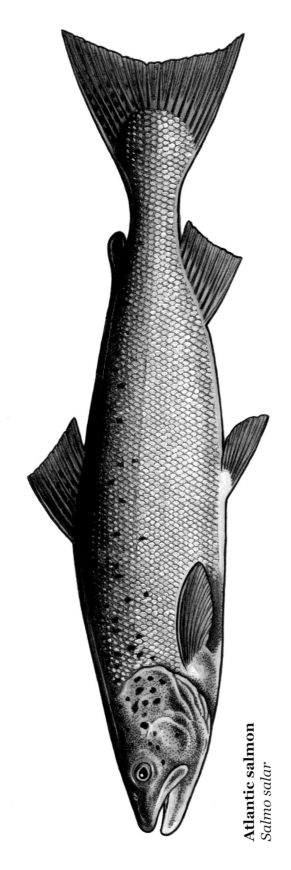

Atlantic salmon
Salmo salar

brown trout
Salmo trutta

rainbow trout
Oncorhynchus mykiss

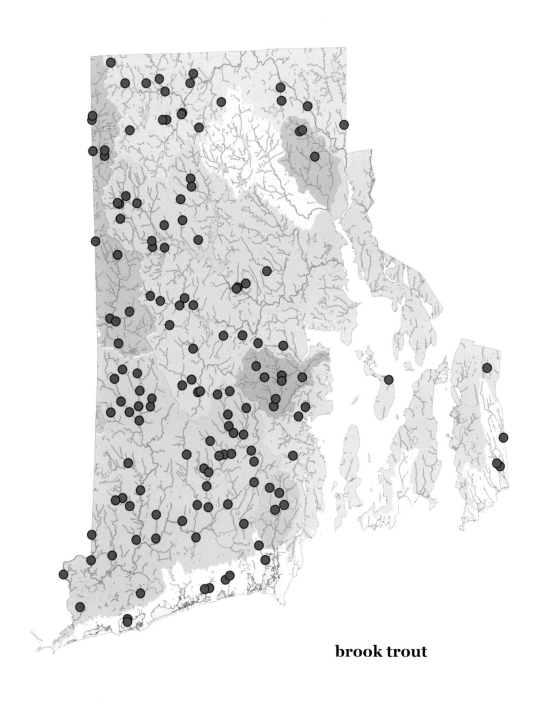

brook trout

brook trout
Salvelinus fontinalis (Mitchill, 1814)

Distribution: This colorful, native fish was the sixth most widely distributed species collected, occurring in more than 35 percent of the locations sampled and in nine out of the ten drainages. Wild brook trout were only collected in streams, whereas brook trout that had been stocked by the state for its put-and-take fisheries were also collected in ponds. Brook trout are endemic to much of eastern North America from Hudson Bay drainages to Newfoundland and south through the Great Lakes basin and the Appalachian Mountains to Georgia. They have been introduced elsewhere and are now widely distributed outside of their natural range.

Identification: Brook trout, sometimes referred to as brook char, are distinguished from other salmonids in Rhode Island by light markings on a dark body. The color of a brook trout is variable; it can be either greenish or brownish in color and covered with light wavy, worm-like lines (vermiculations). Light spots appear on the sides below the vermiculations. Red spots surrounded by a light blue halo may also be apparent. The lower half of the body is tinted orange and during the fall spawning season the orange color in males intensifies. The brilliant white leading edges of the lower fins are a distinguishing characteristic, which can be viewed from above the surface of the water. Young brook trout, which may reach lengths of approximately 7 inches (178 mm), can be distinguished from adults by dark vertical bands (parr marks) located on their sides. These marks fade as they grow. The large mouth of a brook trout parr distinguishes it from a salmon parr. The maxillary of the brook trout parr extends beyond the back edge of the eye, whereas the maxillary of the Atlantic salmon parr is smaller and does not extend beyond the eye.

Remarks: Brook trout inhabiting the Great Lakes are often referred to as "coasters" because of their habit of migrating into coastal streams to spawn. Anadromous brook trout, often referred to as "salters," are found along the east coast of North America from Massachusetts north to Hudson Bay. Not all brook trout inhabiting coastal streams are migratory. Both resident and migratory fish can be found in the same drainage. This carnivorous fish feeds on a variety of invertebrates and fish.

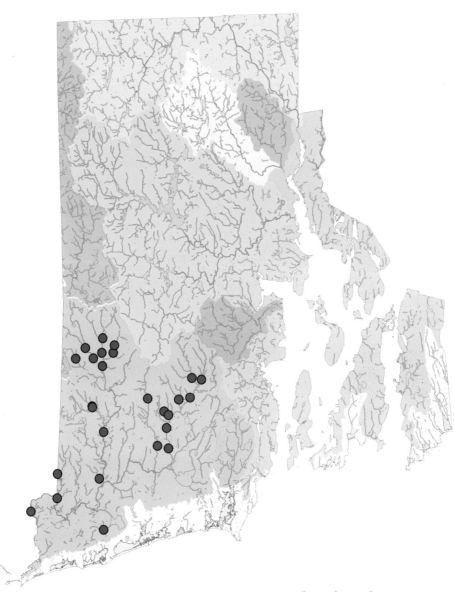

Atlantic salmon

Atlantic salmon
Salmo salar Linnaeus, 1758

Distribution: This native anadromous species was primarily extirpated from Rhode Island by the construction of dams. Dams created barriers to salmon that were returning to natal streams to spawn. In an effort to reestablish a self-sustaining population of Atlantic salmon, salmon fry and smolts are now routinely stocked in the headwaters of the Pawcatuck River drainage, where they grow for one to three years before migrating downstream to the sea. Adults returning to the Pawcatuck River to spawn are 2 to 3 feet (61 – 91 cm) in length and have spent one to three years at sea. Returning adults are trapped at the Potter Hill fishway and are then taken to a hatchery, where they are held until the fall for spawning. Historical accounts show that Atlantic salmon were also found in the Blackstone and Pawtuxet Rivers (CIF 1872; Buckley and Nixon 2001). Atlantic salmon are found in the western Atlantic Ocean from the Connecticut River north through eastern Canada, to southern Greenland and in the eastern Atlantic from Portugal to the Arctic Circle.

Identification: The color of an Atlantic salmon varies with life stage. When young salmon are ready to emigrate they lose their olive color and parr markings and become silvery in color. At this stage they are referred to as smolts and are approximately 5 to 7 inches (127 – 178 mm) in length. Adult salmon entering freshwater to spawn are silvery-white except for their back, which is darker in color. Black spots are found on both the back and sides, but unlike the brown trout, a closely related species, there are generally no red spots on the body of adults. The color of adult salmon varies with the time spent in freshwater and over time it turns various shades of bronze or brown. Red spots may develop on the head and body of adults ready to spawn. Young salmon appear very similar to young brook trout but are easily distinguished from the young trout by the length of the maxillary. The maxillary of young salmon is short and does not extend beyond the rear of the eye as it does on brook trout.

Remarks: Young salmon feed on a variety of aquatic and terrestrial invertebrates when in freshwater and at sea they feed on a variety of fish and crustaceans. Adults do not normally feed during their spawning runs, although they are apt to strike an angler's fly or lure.

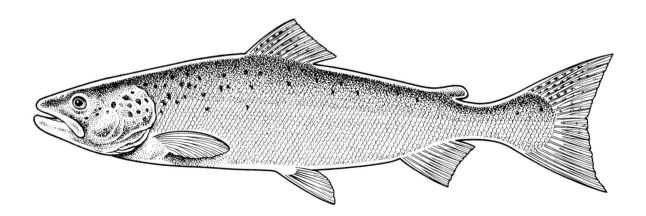

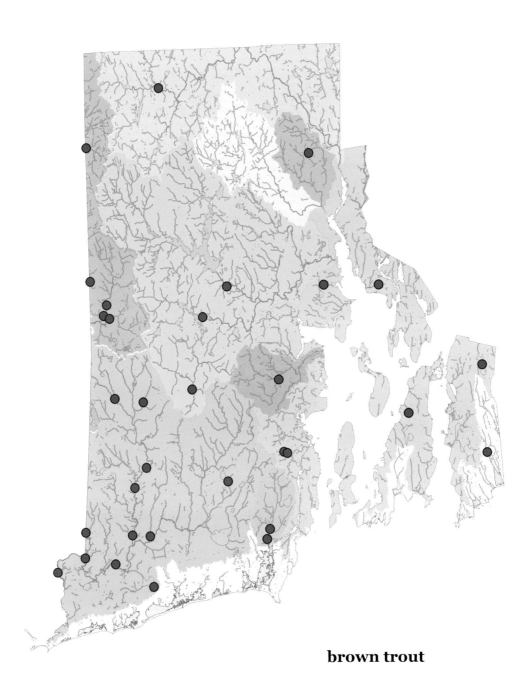

brown trout

brown trout
Salmo trutta Linnaeus, 1758

Distribution: Brown trout are native to Europe and western Asia but were introduced to Rhode Island in 1914. They are stocked annually in selected ponds and streams by the Division for its put-and-take fishery. Naturalized populations were not discovered during the survey, but efforts to establish a sea-run fishery are underway.

Identification: As its name implies, the brown trout is dusky brown dorsally, fading to a lighter color ventrally. As habitat and diet influences color, the brown shading can be variable. Like its close relative the Atlantic salmon, brown trout have dark spots on a light background. Interspersed among the black spots are red or orange spots. Spots are often surrounded by a light halo. Unlike the Atlantic salmon, the maxillary extends well beyond the rear of the eye.

Remarks: The diet of the brown trout consists of invertebrates and fish.

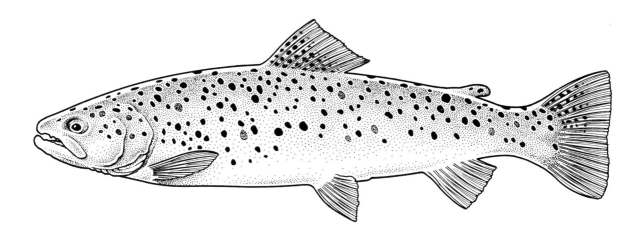

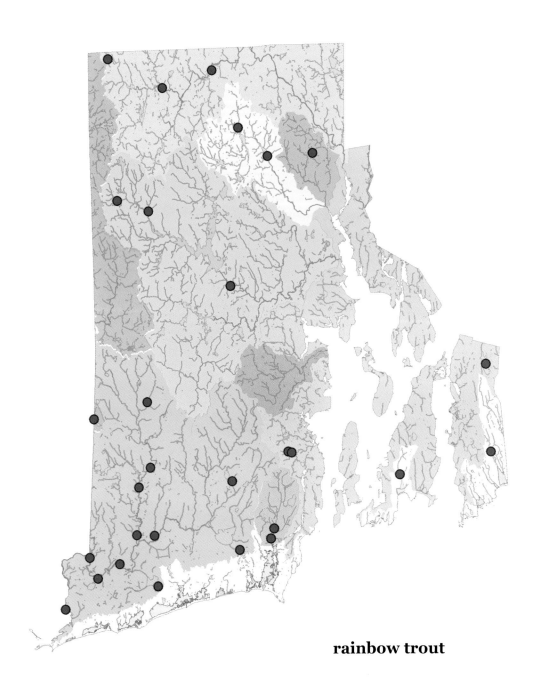

rainbow trout

rainbow trout
Oncorhynchus mykiss (Walbaum, 1792)

Distribution: The rainbow trout is native to western North America from Alaska to Mexico and was introduced into Rhode Island's waters in 1922. Both anadromous and freshwater populations are found in its native range. Rainbow trout are stocked annually in selected ponds and streams by the Division for its put-and-take fishery. Naturalized populations were not discovered during the survey.

Identification: Like the Atlantic salmon and brown trout, rainbow trout have dark spots on a light colored body. Furthermore, unlike the brown trout, it has no red spots on its body. A pinkish lateral band along its sides distinguishes this species from other salmonids in Rhode Island.

Remarks: Rainbow trout feed on fish and a variety of invertebrates, both terrestrial and aquatic.

Cods
Family Gadidae

Cods are primarily demersal marine species that occur in northern latitudes. These fish are characteristically elongate and may have three dorsal fins, one or two anal fins, and a single barbel located near the tip of the lower jaw. Many of the sixteen species found in North America are commercially important.

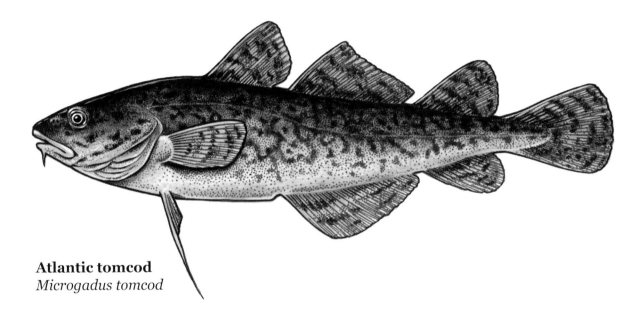

Atlantic tomcod
Microgadus tomcod

Atlantic tomcod

Atlantic tomcod
Microgadus tomcod (Walbaum, 1792)

Distribution: The Atlantic tomcod is a native species that was collected in the tidal portions of the Pawcatuck River and Mill Creek. It is a coastal species that is distributed along eastern North America from Labrador to Virginia.

Identification: Atlantic tomcod are characterized by three dorsal fins, two anal fins, long, tapering pelvic fins, and a single barbel located near the tip of the lower jaw. Dusky olive mottling occurs on the body and fins. Ventral surfaces tend to be white. Few Atlantic tomcod reach lengths of more than 9 to 12 inches (229 – 305 mm).

Remarks: This relatively small edible fish feeds on a variety of small crustaceans, mollusks, polychaete worms, and fish. Spawning generally takes place from November to February in coastal streams and ponds.

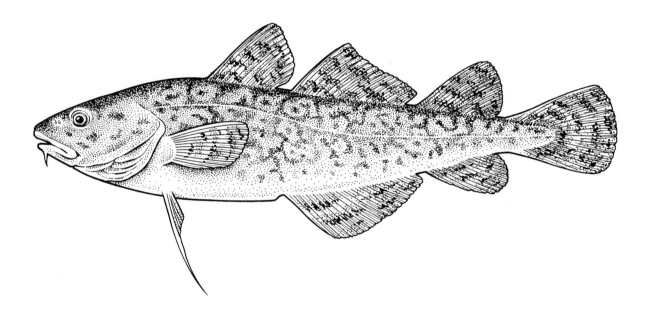

Mullets
Family Mugilidae

This family, consisting primarily of marine and estuarine species, is distributed worldwide in warm waters. The mullet is characterized by an elongated body, the absence of a lateral line, and two widely spaced dorsal fins. The first dorsal fin is spiny and the second is soft-rayed. Among the twelve species found in North America, only one species was collected during the survey.

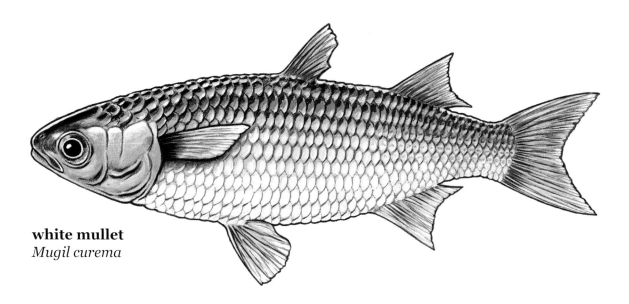

white mullet
Mugil curema

white mullet

white mullet
Mugil curema Valenciennes, 1836

Distribution: The white mullet is a native species that is distributed along the Atlantic Coast from Massachusetts to Brazil. Juveniles approximately 5 inches (127 mm) long are occasionally collected in the lower Pawcatuck River during the fall.

Identification: White mullet, reaching lengths of 15 inches (381 mm), are silvery fish that are darkly shaded dorsally and white ventrally. A yellow or bronze blotch is often found on either side of its head. Pectoral fins are short, not reaching the first dorsal fin, and are located at a point just above the midline. The anal fin has 3 spines and 9 rays. The striped mullet (*Mugil cephalus*), which is also found in coastal waters (Powell 2001), has prominent stripes along its sides and an anal fin with 3 spines and 8 rays. (The convention when counting rays in dorsal and anal fins is to count the last 2 rays as one in this family and certain others.)

Remarks: Mullets feed on a variety of plant and animal material.

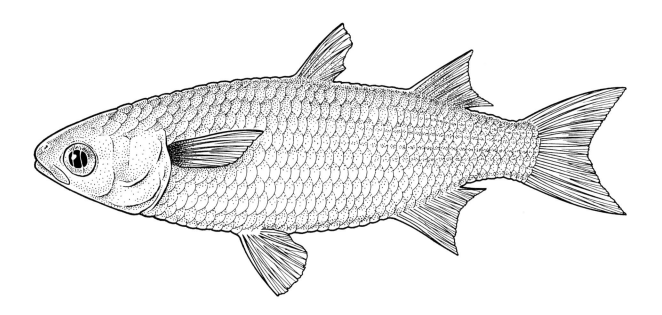

New World Silversides
Family Atherinopsidae

These slender elongated fish are somewhat transparent and possess a pronounced silvery stripe along each side and two widely spaced dorsal fins. The first dorsal fin is smaller and less conspicuous than the second. The head contains a distinctive upturned mouth and large eyes. Fifty-six species are found in North America in both offshore and inshore habitats.

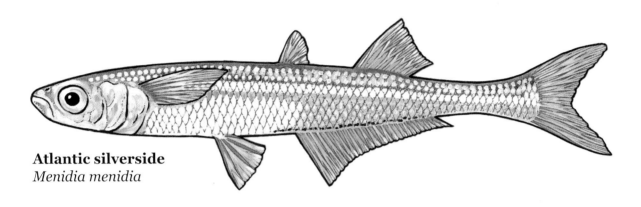

Atlantic silverside
Menidia menidia

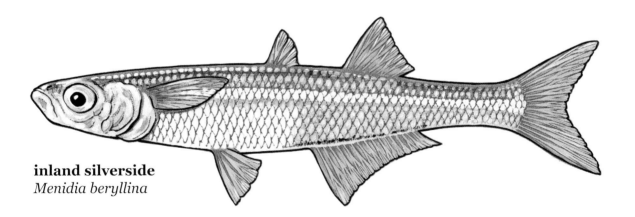

inland silverside
Menidia beryllina

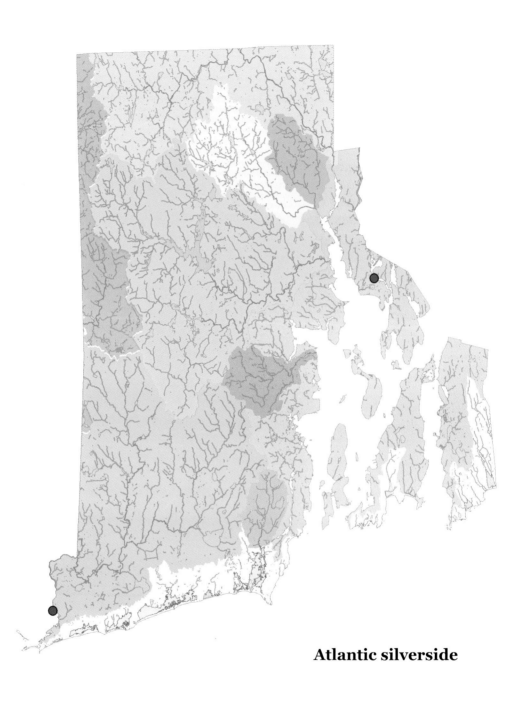

Atlantic silverside

Atlantic silverside
Menidia menidia (Linnaeus, 1766)

Distribution: The Atlantic silverside is a native fish that is occasionally collected in the brackish water regions of the lower Pawcatuck River and in a stream that flows out of Prince Pond. The Atlantic silverside is a coastal fish that ranges from the Gulf of St. Lawrence to Florida. It is commonly found in bays and estuaries, occasionally entering freshwater.

Identification: The Atlantic silverside is slightly longer than the inland silverside, averaging approximately 4 to 4.5 inches (102 – 114 mm) in length. Specimens ranging in length from approximately 1 to 4 inches (25 – 102 mm) were caught during the survey. Atlantic silversides are a translucent greenish-gray color with a distinct silvery lateral band along the sides. Large eyes and an oblique mouth are also characteristic. This species and the inland silverside are very similar in appearance. The longer base of the anal fin, having more than 22 rays, readily distinguishes it from the inland silverside.

Remarks: This omnivore feeds chiefly on aquatic invertebrates and fish eggs and in turn serves as forage for a number of species such striped bass and bluefish.

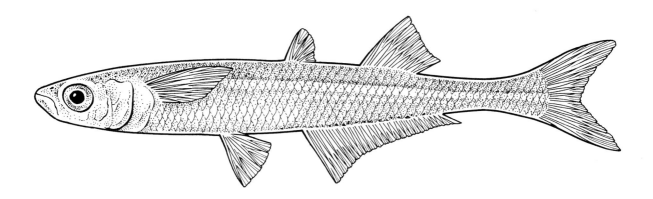

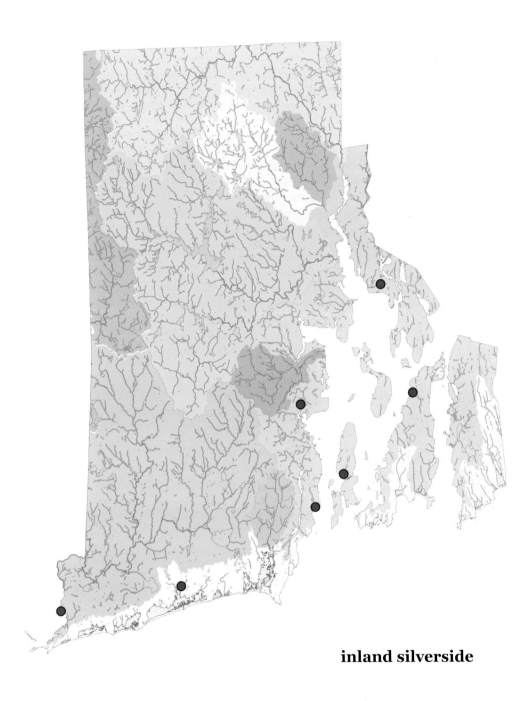

inland silverside

inland silverside
Menidia beryllina (Cope, 1867)

Distribution: This native fish was collected from several freshwater and brackish water locations. The inland silverside occurs along the Atlantic Coast from Massachusetts to Mexico. They are frequently found swimming in schools in bays, salt marshes, and freshwater areas.

Identification: The inland silverside is smaller than the Atlantic silverside, averaging approximately 3 inches (76 mm) in length. Fish ranging from approximately 0.5 to 3 inches (13 – 76 mm) in length were collected. The inland silverside is very similar in appearance to the Atlantic silverside. The grayish translucent body has a pale yellow-green cast with a distinct silvery lateral band along the sides. Large eyes and an oblique mouth are also apparent. The shorter base of the anal fin, having fewer than 22 rays, distinguishes this species from the Atlantic silverside.

Remarks: The diet of the inland silverside is similar to the Atlantic silverside and includes small fish, worms, etc. It is also an important prey item for larger fish as well as a common bait fish.

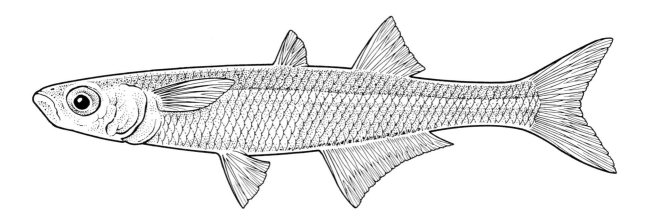

Needlefishes
Family Belonidae

Members of this family are found in freshwater and marine habitats in the Atlantic, Pacific, and Indian Oceans. Needlefish are long and slender with elongated jaws that form a bill. Ten species are found in North America.

Atlantic needlefish
Strongylura marina

150   Atlantic needlefish

Atlantic needlefish
Strongylura marina (Walbaum, 1792)

Distribution: This slender marine species is occasionally collected in the brackish water of the lower Pawcatuck River. The Atlantic needlefish ranges along the Atlantic and Gulf Coasts from Maine to Texas but is most common in the southern part of its range.

Identification: Although reaching lengths of approximately 24 inches (610 mm), specimens that exceeded 12 inches (305 mm) in length were rarely collected. Atlantic needlefish are generally greenish-blue dorsally and silvery below. A long dark lateral stripe may occur along its sides. The dorsal and anal fins are located near the rear of the body. The needlefish is equipped with long slender jaws containing many teeth. The tip of the lower jaw extends slightly beyond the upper jaw.

Remarks: This predator feeds on a variety of small fish.

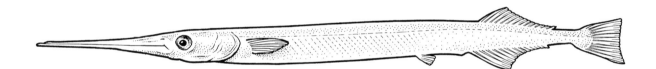

Topminnows
Family Fundulidae

Forty species in this family occur throughout North America. Topminnows, often seen swimming at or near the surface of the water, occupy a wide variety of habitats ranging from freshwater to marine. They are also able to tolerate a wide variety of other environmental conditions, including large variations in temperature and oxygen concentrations. A conspicuously flattened head and a lower jaw that usually extends beyond the upper jaw enables a topminnow to respire and feed at the water's surface. The fins lack spines and the single dorsal fin and caudal fin are rounded. Coloration is usually different between males and females. Many are commonly used as bait in recreational fishing.

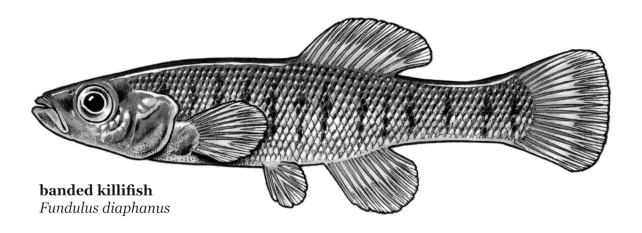

banded killifish
Fundulus diaphanus

mummichog
Fundulus heteroclitus

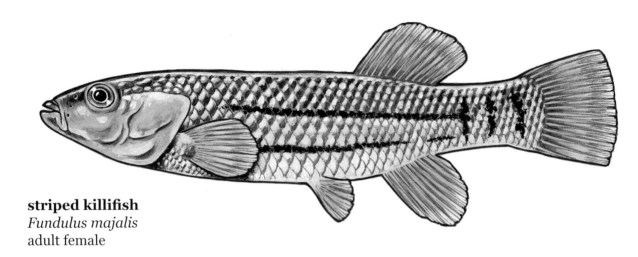

striped killifish
Fundulus majalis
adult female

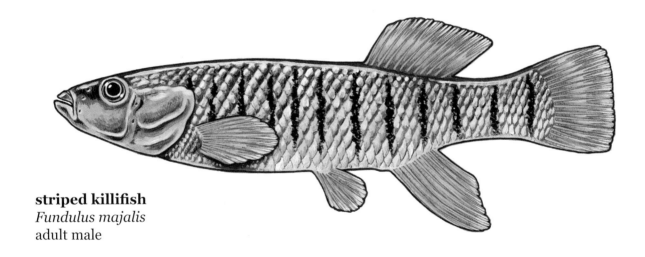

striped killifish
Fundulus majalis
adult male

rainwater killifish
Lucania parva

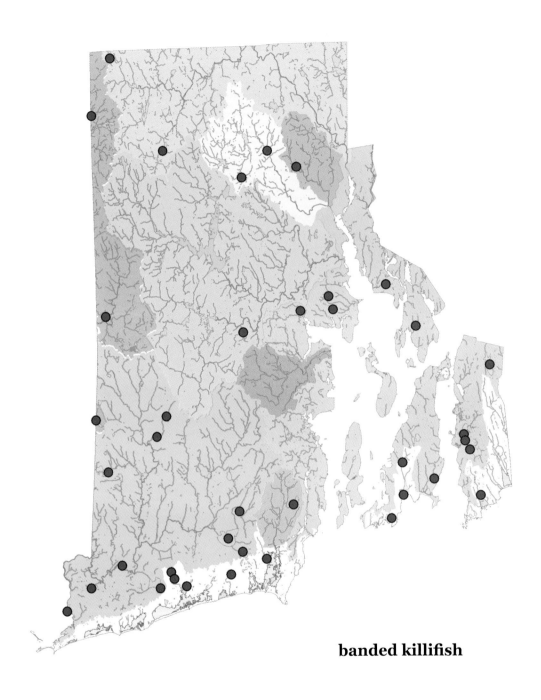

banded killifish

banded killifish
Fundulus diaphanus (Lesueur, 1817)

Distribution: The banded killifish is a native species found throughout the state, primarily in freshwater locations. More of these small fish were collected from ponds than streams. They may occasionally be seen swimming in schools in the shallow sandy areas along the shores of ponds and streams. The banded killifish is found, for the most part, in freshwater from Newfoundland to South Carolina and west to Montana.

Identification: This species, seldom more than 3.5 inches (89 mm) in length, is olive gray to dark brown in color dorsally, fading to a pale white below. There are dark vertical bars on the sides of the fish. For males, the sides are silvery with numerous dark vertical bars, whereas females lack the silvery sides of males and have fewer vertical bars. During the spawning period the color of males intensifies, with shades of blue appearing on the body. The banded killifish is more slender than the mummichog and has more mid-lateral scales (>40). The position of the dorsal fin, located closer to the head on the banded killifish than on the mummichog, is also useful to distinguish between these two similar appearing species (see page 153). For the banded killifish, the distance between the origin of the dorsal fin and the middle of the eye is about equal to the distance from the origin of the dorsal fin to the base of the caudal fin.

Remarks: This fish is primarily carnivorous, feeding on a variety of small organisms. In turn, it is preyed upon by other fish species and is frequently used as bait by anglers.

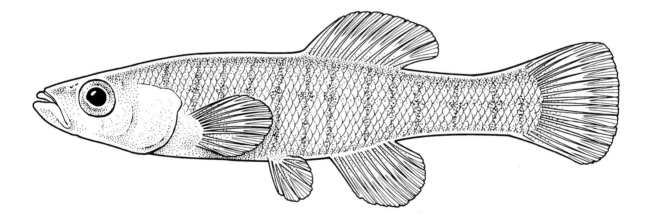

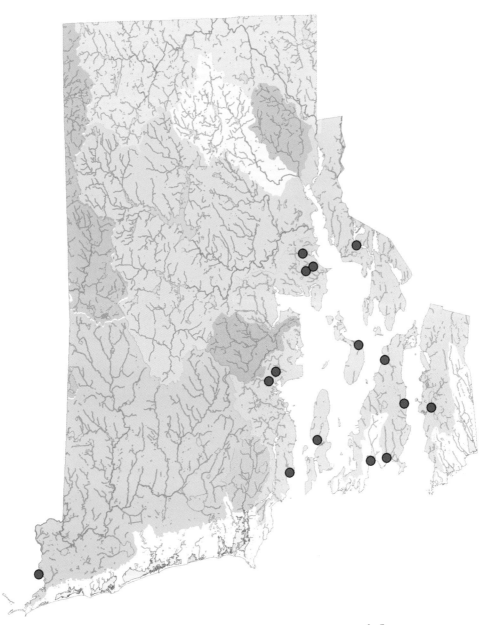

mummichog

mummichog
Fundulus heteroclitus (Linnaeus, 1766)

Distribution: This native species was collected in both fresh and brackish locations. These small fish were never collected very far from brackish water. The mummichog is found in sheltered coastal waters from Newfoundland to Florida, most commonly occurring in salt marshes and tidal creeks.

Identification: Coloration is highly variable but is generally olive dorsally and pale white or yellow below. Faint vertical bands or bars generally occur along its sides. Males tend to be more colorful than females during the spawning season, having silvery vertical bands on their sides and shades of yellow on the lower fins. Scales may have white or yellow spots. The mummichog is more robust and has fewer mid-lateral scales (<39) than the banded killifish. The position of the dorsal fin, located closer to the tail on the mummichog than on the banded killifish, is also a useful aid to distinguish between these two similar species (see page 153). For the mummichog, the distance between the origin of the dorsal fin and the middle of the eye is more than the distance from the origin of the dorsal fin to the base of the caudal fin. Specimens that were captured rarely exceeded 3.5 inches (89 mm) in length.

Remarks: The mummichog is very tolerant of large fluctuations in temperature, oxygen, and salinity. This omnivore feeds on a variety of plant material and animals, including small fish, fish eggs, crustaceans, etc. It is also a popular bait fish with anglers.

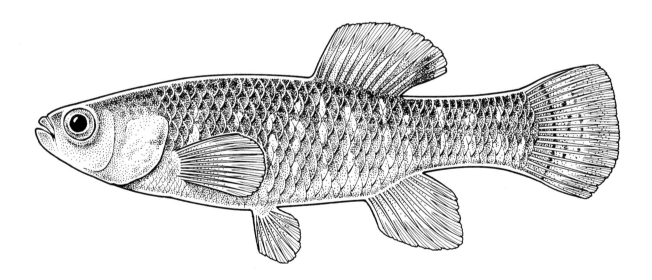

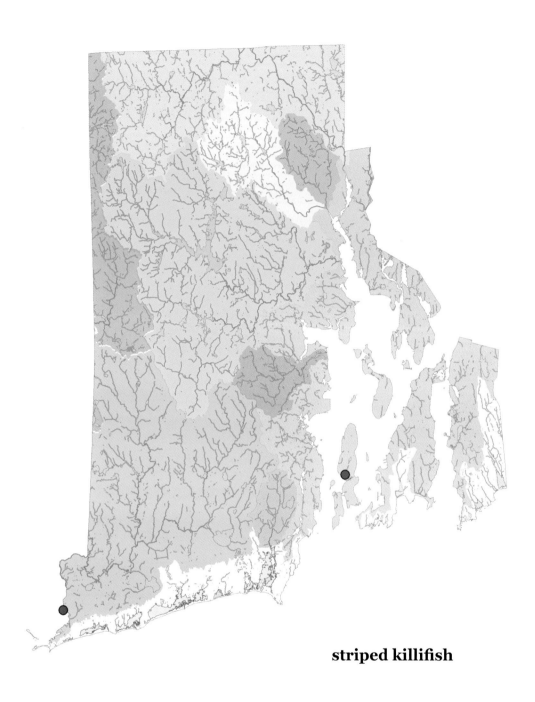

striped killifish

striped killifish
Fundulus majalis (Walbaum, 1792)

Distribution: The striped killifish is a native species that was collected from two brackish water locations. It is commonly found in protected areas along the Atlantic Coast from New Hampshire to Florida.

Identification: The striped killifish grows larger than any of the other topminnows collected and may reach lengths of 6 to 7 inches (152-178 mm). This fish is generally olive or grayish in color dorsally and whitish below. Color patterns easily distinguish males from females in mature fish. Adult males have dark vertical bars along the sides, whereas adult females have two or three longitudinal stripes on each side. Similar to males, young females also have dark vertical bars, which become longitudinal as the fish grows older. The large head of the striped killifish, nearly a third of its standard length, distinguishes it from the other topminnows.

Remarks: This species feeds on a variety of organisms, including fish, mollusks and crustaceans.

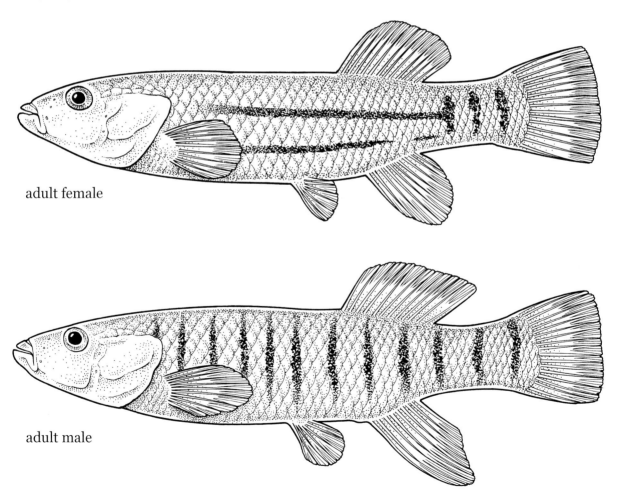

adult female

adult male

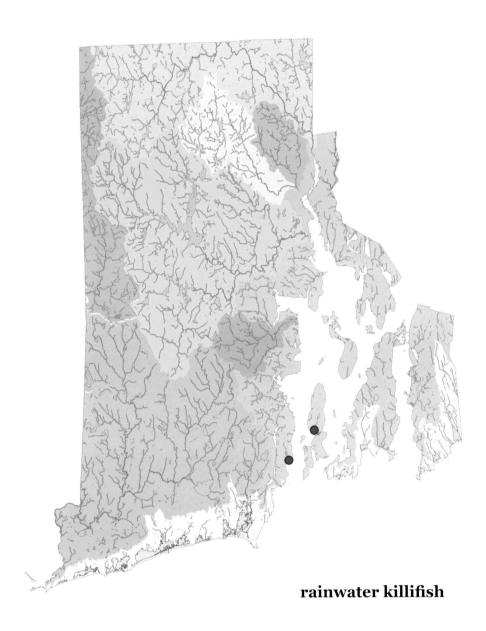

rainwater killifish

rainwater killifish
Lucania parva (Baird & Girard, 1855)

Distribution: This native species was collected from two brackish water locations, Wesquage Pond and Jamestown Brook. The rainwater killifish is found in salt marshes, coves, and tidal creeks along the Atlantic Coast from Massachusetts to Mexico.

Identification: These small fish may reach lengths up to 2.75 inches (70 mm). The rainwater killifish is light brown or tan above and white below with each scale being outlined with a dusky margin. A faint longitudinal band is found along each side.

Remarks: The diet of this small killifish consists of a variety of aquatic invertebrates.

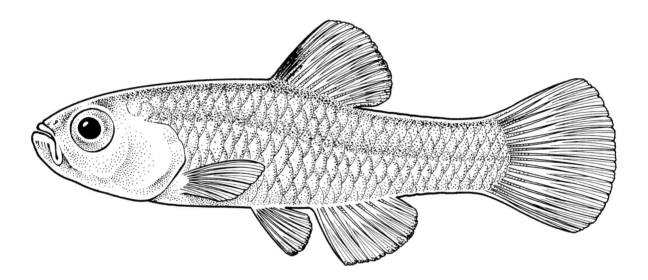

Pupfishes
Family Cyprinodontidae

Forty-four species of this family occur in North America. Like topminnows, pupfishes have upturned mouths and a single rounded dorsal fin. They are also able to tolerate a wide variety of environmental conditions. Unlike topminnows, many pupfishes are deep-bodied.

sheepshead minnow
Cyprinodon variegatus

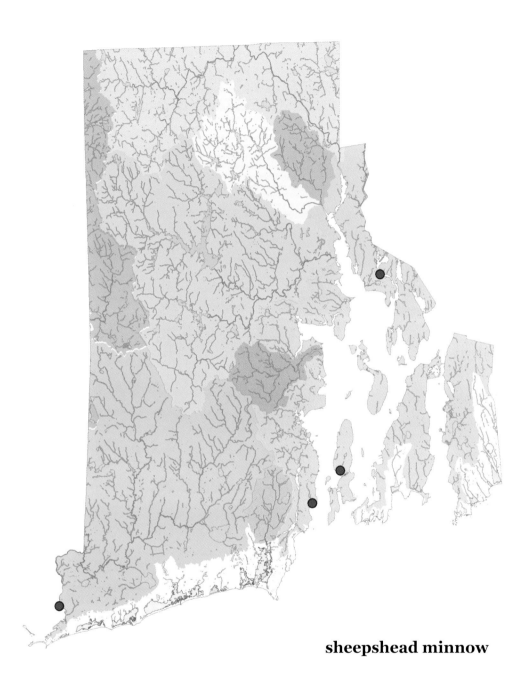

sheepshead minnow

sheepshead minnow
Cyprinodon variegatus Lacepede, 1803

Distribution: This native species was collected in four brackish water locations. The sheepshead minnow is distributed along the East Coast of North America from Massachusetts to Mexico in shallow fresh, brackish, or saltwater coves and inlets.

Identification: The sheepshead minnow is a deep-bodied, robust fish that may reach 3 inches (76 mm) in length. Unlike topminnows, the pectoral fins of this species extend beyond the origin of the dorsal fin. The teeth of sheepshead minnows are flattened and have two or three cusps (points), whereas the teeth of the rainwater killifish, banded killifish, mummichog, and striped killifish are conical. The dorsal surface of a sheepshead minnow is generally dark brown to olive in color. There are dark irregular vertical bands on the sides of the body. Males have a distinctive dark edge on their caudal fin and during the spawning period the ventral surface of mature males may be salmon-colored.

Remarks: The sheepshead minnow is omnivorous, feeding on a variety of animal and plant material throughout the water column.

Sticklebacks
Family Gasterosteidae

Sticklebacks are small fish that are characterized by laterally flattened bodies and well-developed spines in the dorsal and pelvic fins. They are found in coastal freshwater, brackish, and marine habitats of North America, Asia, and Europe. Three of the five species that occur in North America were collected in Rhode Island. Freshwater and anadromous populations are believed to exist for some species. During the breeding season the male builds a nest of aquatic vegetation, which it guards until the young swim off.

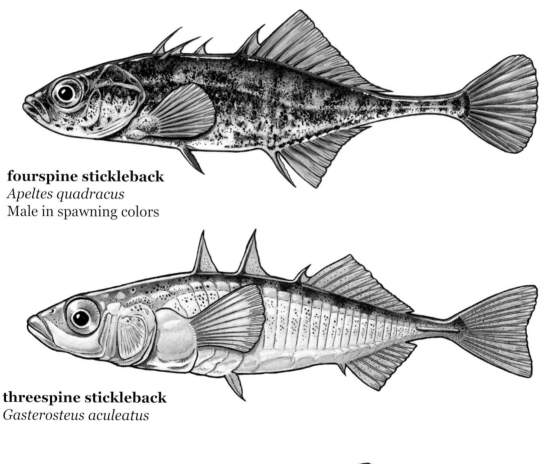

fourspine stickleback
Apeltes quadracus
Male in spawning colors

threespine stickleback
Gasterosteus aculeatus

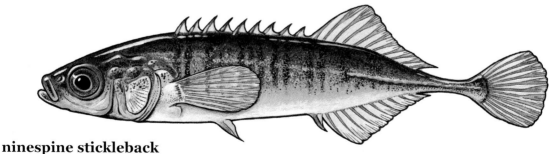

ninespine stickleback
Pungitius pungitius

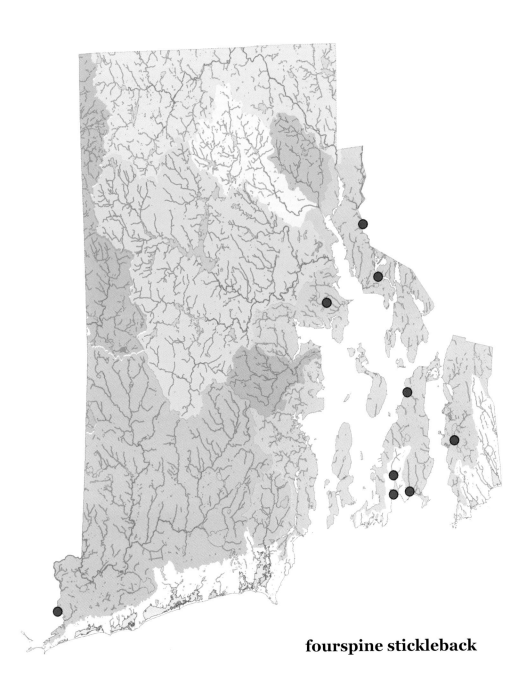

fourspine stickleback

fourspine stickleback
Apeltes quadracus (Mitchill, 1815)

Distribution: This native fish was collected in the fresh and brackish waters of several coastal streams. The fourspine stickleback is found along the Atlantic Coast in marine, brackish, and freshwater locations from Newfoundland to North Carolina.

Identification: Fourspine sticklebacks are generally characterized by four prominent spines located in front of the dorsal fin. These fish are dark brown or olive in color, with mottling along the sides, and silvery white below. Pelvic fins become red in breeding males. Unlike the threespine and ninespine sticklebacks, it lacks bony keels along the caudal peduncle. This small fish may reach a length of 2.5 inches (64 mm).

Remarks: The fourspine stickleback feeds on planktonic organisms, including amphipods and isopods.

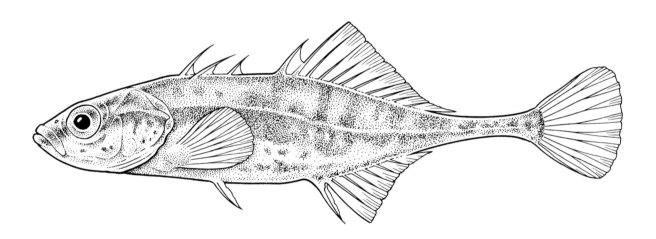

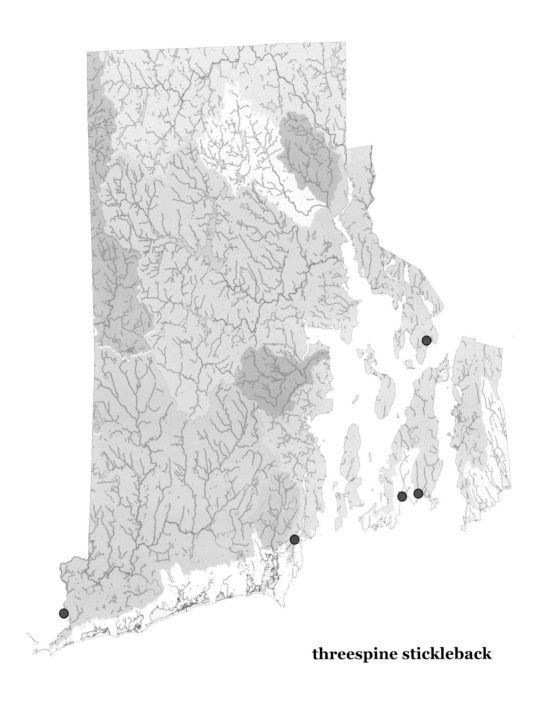

threespine stickleback

threespine stickleback
Gasterosteus aculeatus Linnaeus, 1758

Distribution: The threespine stickleback is a native anadromous species that was collected in the fresh and brackish waters of five coastal streams. This stickleback is widely distributed in salt marshes and creeks of North America. In the Atlantic Ocean, it ranges from Chesapeake Bay to Hudson and Baffin Bays and in the Pacific Ocean from Baja California to Alaska.

Identification: Usually, three prominent dorsal spines are found in front of the dorsal fin on this species. Unlike the fourspine and ninespine sticklebacks, the sides of its body are covered with bony plates. Bony keels are found on either side of the caudal peduncle, similar to the ninespine stickleback. The color is variable, ranging from a grayish color dorsally, to a silvery white on the sides and below. The threespine stickleback is the largest of the three species collected, averaging 2 to 3 inches (51 - 76 mm) in length.

Remarks: The threespine stickleback feeds on a variety of plants and animals, including worms, crustaceans, fish eggs and fry.

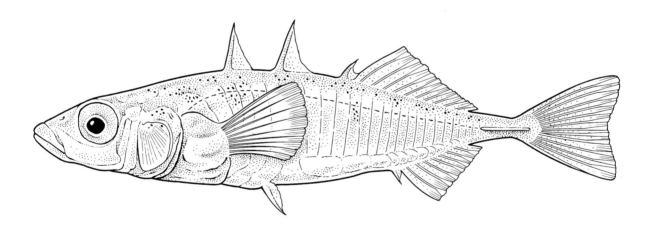

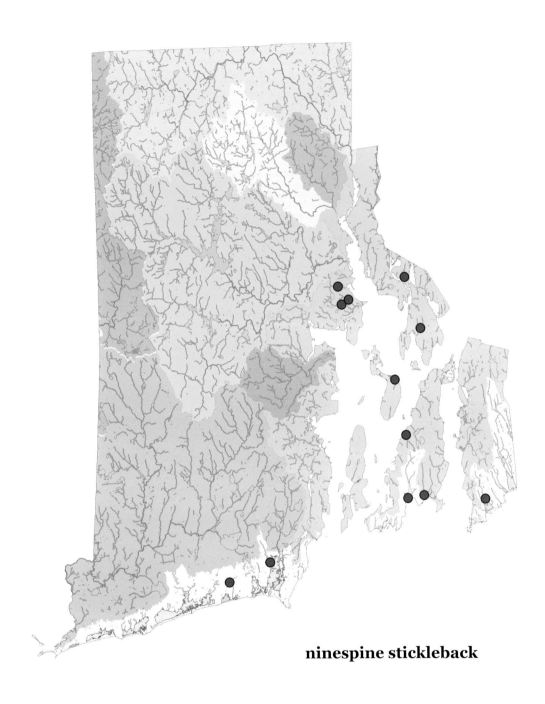

ninespine stickleback

ninespine stickleback
Pungitius pungitius (Linnaeus, 1758)

Distribution: The ninespine stickleback is a native species that was collected primarily in the freshwaters of several coastal streams. It was more widely distributed than the threespine and fourspine sticklebacks. The ninespine stickleback is circumpolar in distribution. In North America it occurs in salt marshes and creeks along Arctic and Atlantic Coast drainages from Alaska, across Canada, to New Jersey.

Identification: Usually, nine alternating spines are found in front of the dorsal fin. Bony keels are found along a slender caudal peduncle. The ninespine stickleback is dusky olive-brown dorsally and pale below, with dark irregular markings along its sides. This stickleback, averaging approximately 2 inches (51 mm) in length, is more slender than the threespine and fourspine sticklebacks.

Remarks: The ninespine stickleback feeds on plants and small aquatic invertebrates, including fish eggs and fry.

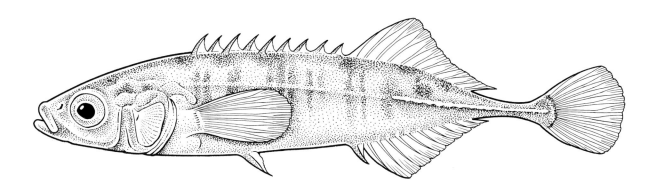

Pipefishes
Family Syngnathidae

This family, which includes seahorses, is found throughout the world in marine and brackish water environments of temperate and tropical oceans. Of the 36 species found in North America, the pipefish was the only member of this family caught during the survey. These long slender fish are characterized by rings of bony plates circling the body, a long tubular snout with a small mouth at the tip, and a rounded caudal fin. Pelvic fins are absent.

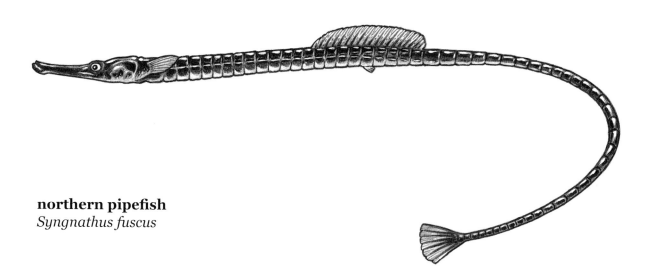

northern pipefish
Syngnathus fuscus

northern pipefish

northern pipefish
Syngnathus fuscus Storer, 1839

Distribution: The northern pipefish is a native species that was collected in the brackish water of the lower Pawcatuck River. It is found along the Atlantic Coast from the Gulf of St. Lawrence south to Florida in salt and brackish water.

Identification: A northern pipefish is long and slender (approximately 30 times as long as it is deep), averaging 4 to 8 inches (102 – 203 mm) in length. Also characteristic are the absence of pelvic fins and the presence of a tiny anal fin on the abdomen in an area below the dorsal fin. They are usually olive or brown in color above, with paler shades below. Depending on the habitat, they may have a noticeable greenish tint.

Remarks: Females deposit their eggs in the male's brood pouch, where they remain after hatching until reaching approximately 0.33 inches (8 mm) in length. Pipefish feed on plankton, especially copepods and amphipods.

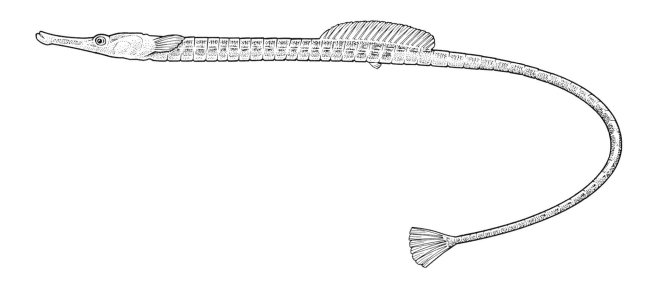

Searobins
Family Triglidae

This family is distributed world-wide in temperate and tropical seas. Twenty-four species are found in North America. Searobins are characterized by a large armored head with numerous ridges and spines and large, wing-like pectoral fins having three detached fingerlike rays lowermost on the fins. These benthic species utilize the fingerlike rays for support and while searching for food.

northern searobin
Prionotus carolinus

northern searobin

northern searobin
Prionotus carolinus (Linnaeus, 1771)

Distribution: Juveniles of this native marine species were found in the brackish water of the lower Pawcatuck River. The northern searobin is a demersal species that occurs along the Atlantic Coast from the Bay of Fundy south to South Carolina.

Identification: The northern searobin, which may reach a length of more than 15 inches (381 mm), is dark gray to reddish-brown in color above and pale below. Spots covering the body of younger fish, approximately 4 inches (102 mm) in length, give way to several dark saddle-like blotches that may appear on the backs of older fish. A prominent black spot on the first dorsal fin distinguishes this species from the striped searobin (*Prionotus evolans*), a species not collected during the survey but also found in the state's coastal waters (Powell 2001).

Remarks: These tasty fish are of minor commercial importance. Northern searobins are bottom-dwelling species that feed on a variety of organisms, including crustaceans, mollusks, and fish.

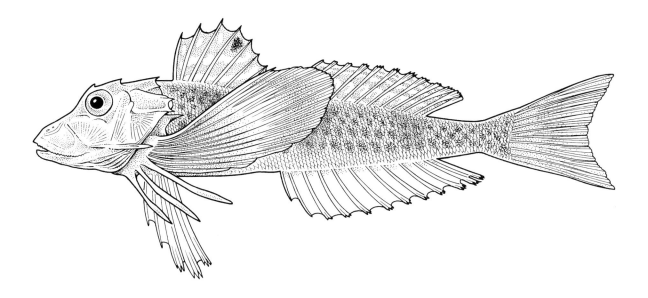

Temperate Basses
Family Moronidae

Temperate basses occupy a wide variety of habitats that range from freshwater to saltwater. They possess two closely placed dorsal fins, a forked caudal fin, and one or two opercular spines. The two species that were caught during the survey, among four that occur in North America, are of commercial and recreational importance.

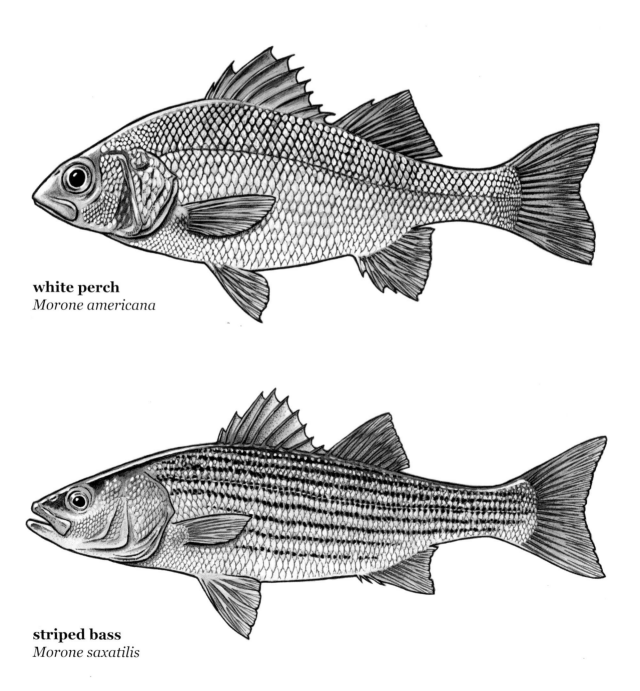

white perch
Morone americana

striped bass
Morone saxatilis

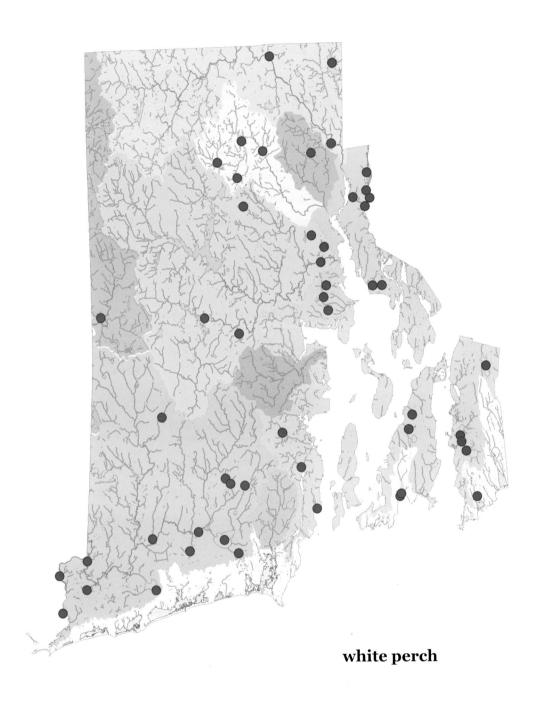

white perch

white perch
Morone americana (Gmelin, 1789)

Distribution: The white perch is a native species that was fairly well-distributed throughout the state, occurring primarily in ponds. This brackish water species can tolerate a wide range of salinities. Landlocked populations were also established throughout the state in early stocking programs. White perch are found along the Atlantic Coast of North America from Nova Scotia to South Carolina.

Identification: White perch are generally dark gray or olive brown dorsally, with silvery sides and white below. This relatively deep-bodied fish lacks the streamlined body and lateral stripes of the striped bass. White perch have two dorsal fins; the first dorsal is located directly above the prominently arched back. Unlike the stripe bass, the three anal spines are not evenly graduated, with the second spine nearly as long as the third (see below). White perch living entirely in freshwater do not tend to grow as large as brackish water populations. Few white perch were collected that were longer than 12 inches (305 mm).

Remarks: White perch, considered by some to be anadromous, feed on a variety of organisms that include aquatic insects and small fish.

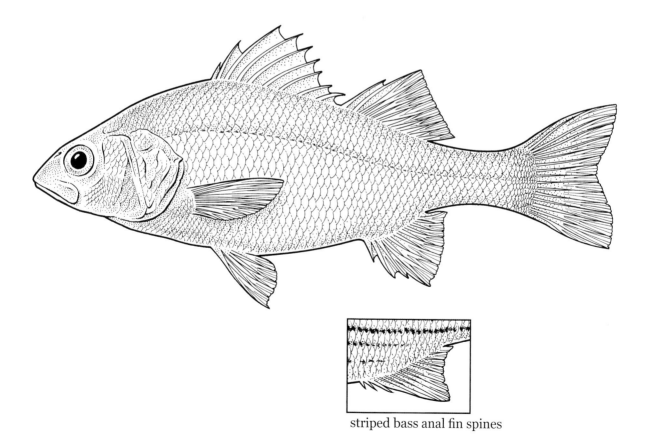

striped bass anal fin spines

striped bass

striped bass
Morone saxatilis (Walbaum, 1792)

Distribution: The striped bass is a native, anadromous species that was collected in the lower Pawcatuck and Saugatucket Rivers. Bass as long as 18 inches (457 mm) are often collected in the lower Pawcatuck during routine surveys. Striped bass are native to the Atlantic Coast of North America, occurring from the St. Lawrence River and Nova Scotia to Florida and the Gulf of Mexico. Spawning takes place in the southern part of its range and is believed not to occur in Rhode Island waters. It has been successfully introduced to the West Coast of North America.

Identification: The striped bass is a large popular game fish that often exceeds 40 inches (102 cm) in length and 50 pounds (23 kg) in weight. Depending on its surroundings, striped bass are often steel blue, brown, olive, or greenish dorsally, with seven or eight dark stripes on silvery sides and white below. Two closely placed dorsal fins occur on a streamlined body. Unlike the white perch, the three anal spines are evenly graduated (see below).

Remarks: Striped bass are voracious feeders whose diets include a variety of animals such as fish and crustaceans. Overfishing and environmental degradation led to the collapse of the fishery in the 1980s, but management regulations have allowed stocks to rebound.

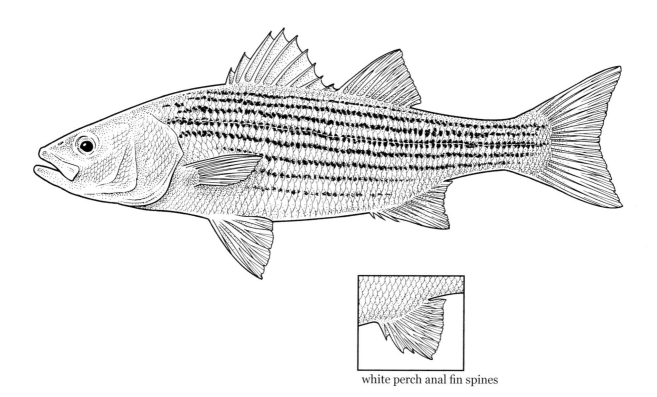

white perch anal fin spines

Sunfishes
Family Centrarchidae

Indigenous to the freshwaters of North America, many in this family, which includes black bass (genus *Micropterus*), crappie, and sunfish, have now been introduced to areas where they did not originally occur. A large number of the 31 species in this family are colorful and important to recreational fisheries. Most have deep, laterally compressed bodies and two dorsal fins that contain spines and rays that are connected by membranes. During the breeding season males build nests in the sand or gravel by vigorously fanning the water with their fins. After spawning, males guard their nests until the fry disperse. Seven species were collected during the survey.

banded sunfish
Enneacanthus obesus

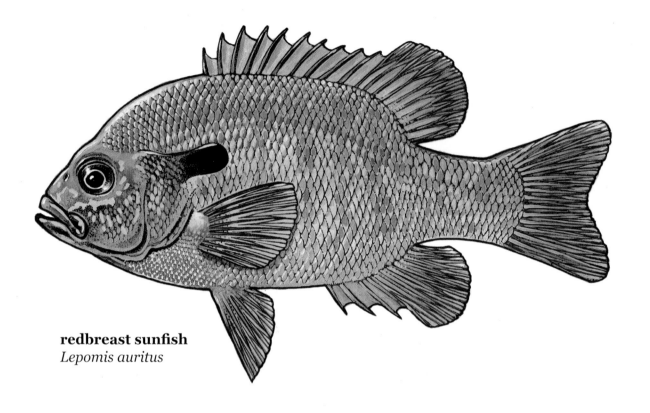

redbreast sunfish
Lepomis auritus

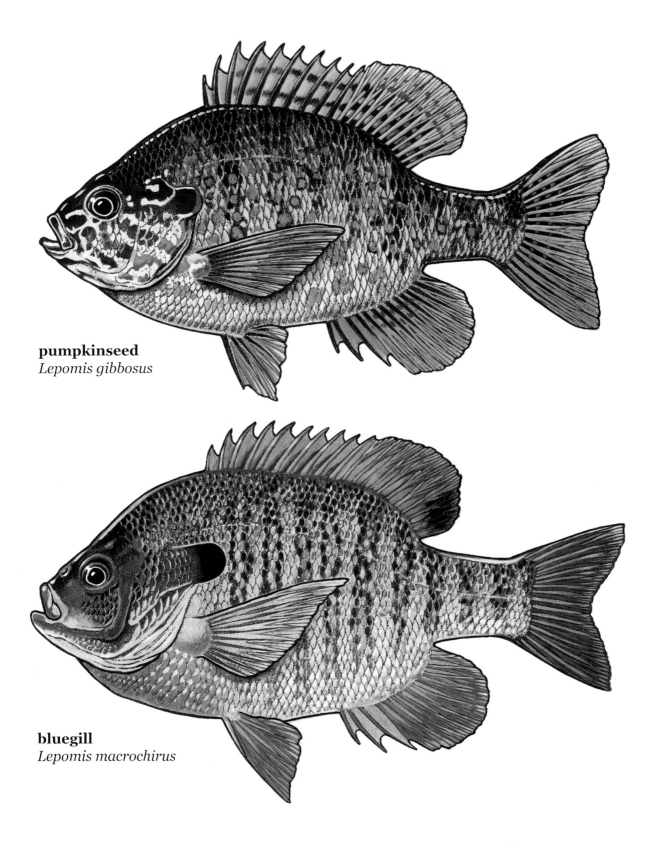

pumpkinseed
Lepomis gibbosus

bluegill
Lepomis macrochirus

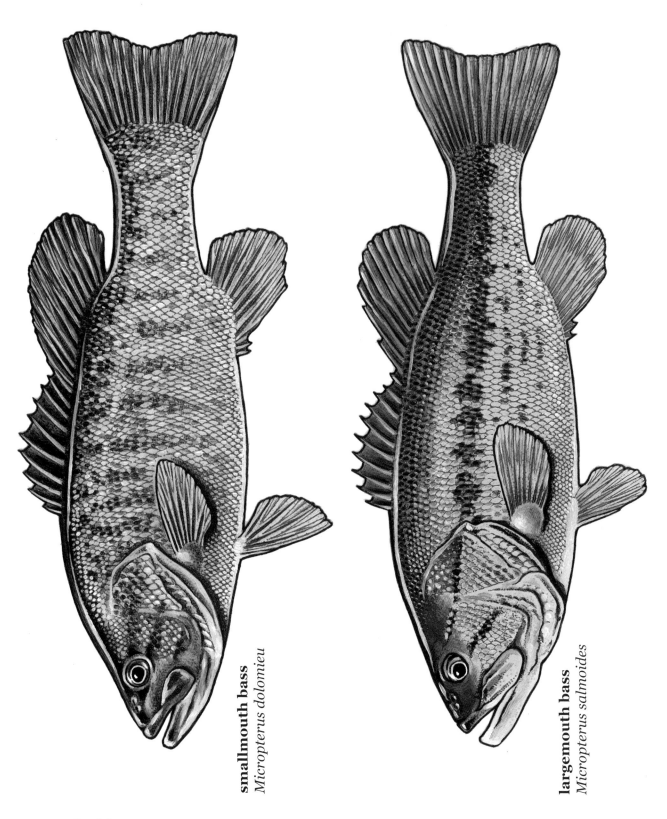

smallmouth bass
Micropterus dolomieu

largemouth bass
Micropterus salmoides

black crappie
Pomoxis nigromaculatus

Sunfishes 195

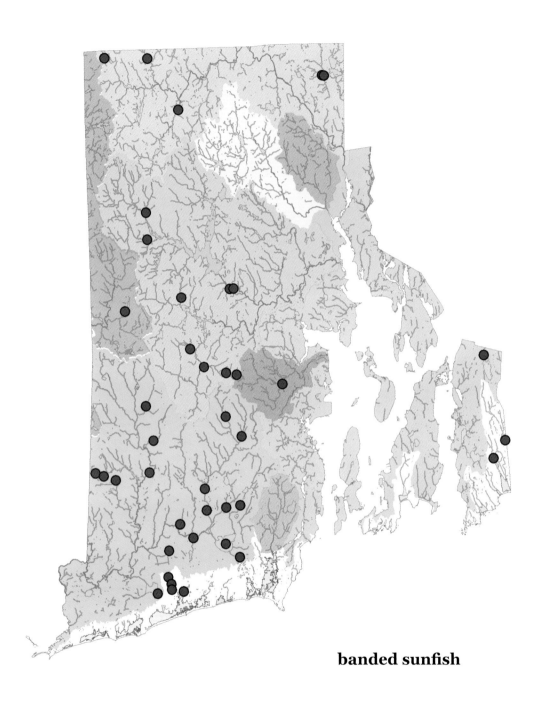

banded sunfish

banded sunfish
Enneacanthus obesus (Girard, 1854)

Distribution: The banded sunfish is a small native species that was found in several localities scattered throughout the state. The banded sunfish is generally found in sluggish, heavily vegetated waters from New Hampshire to Florida.

Identification: The banded sunfish is olive-brown in color with several dark vertical bars along its sides. Its sides are also covered with iridescent brass, white or blue spots. This robust little fish reaches lengths of approximately 3.75 inches (95 mm). It is the only member of this family occurring in Rhode Island waters having a rounded caudal fin.

Remarks: The banded sunfish feeds on a variety of small aquatic invertebrates such as copepods and amphipods.

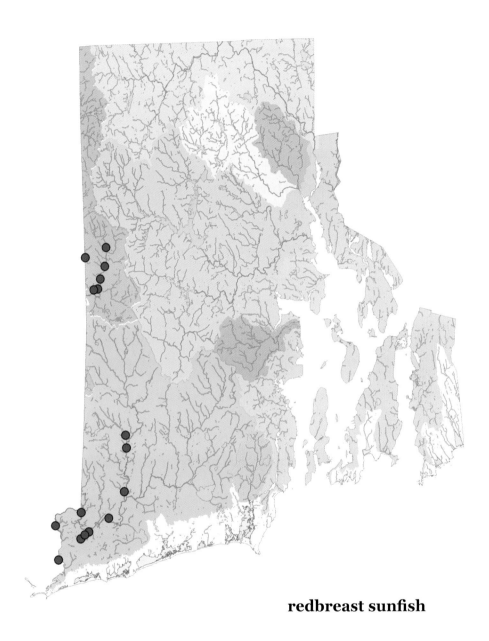

redbreast sunfish

redbreast sunfish
Lepomis auritus (Linnaeus, 1758)

Distribution: The redbreast sunfish is a native species whose distribution was limited to the western portion of the state. It was collected primarily from the rocky and gravelly areas of both streams and ponds. It is native to Atlantic Slope drainages from New Brunswick to Florida.

Identification: Redbreast sunfish rarely exceed 8.5 inches (216 mm) in length. They are generally olive-brown dorsally, becoming lighter and bluish lower along the sides. The breast is orange or red. Orange-brown or orange spots may occur along the sides. The fins, especially the tail, are frequently tinged with red. Blue wavy streaks occur in the area around the snout and eyes. Vertical bars or stripes are more noticeable on younger fish. The opercular flap is long in older fish and all black. The pectoral fins are short and rounded in comparison to the long pointed pectoral fins of the pumpkinseed and bluegill. When folded forward they barely reach the eye.

Remarks: The diet of the redbreast sunfish consists of a variety of aquatic invertebrates and small fish.

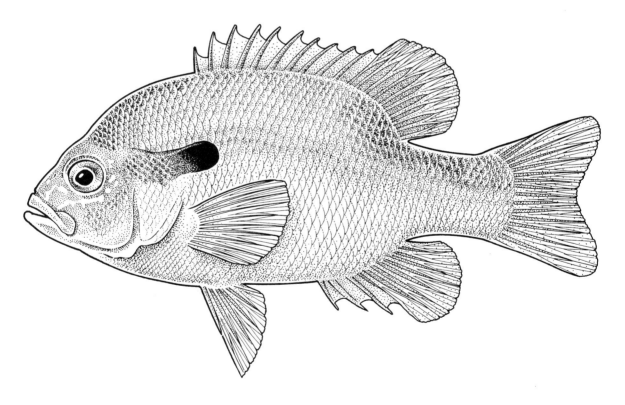

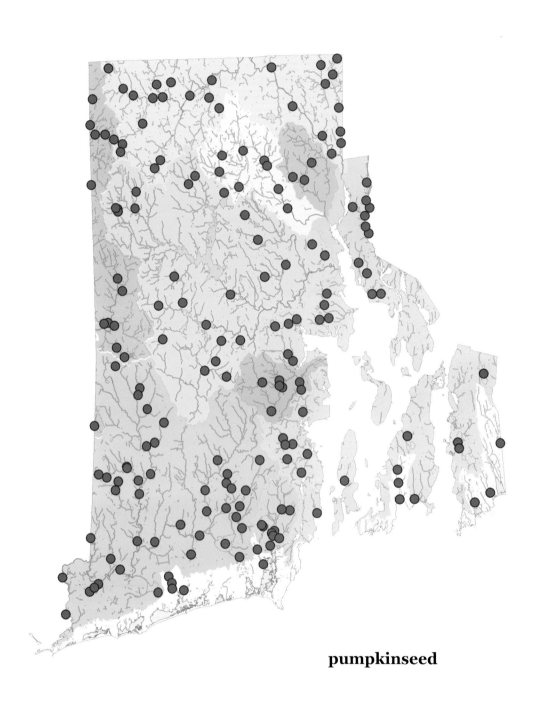

pumpkinseed

pumpkinseed
Lepomis gibbosus (Linnaeus, 1758)

Distribution: The pumpkinseed is a native freshwater fish that was the third most widely-distributed species collected. It occurred in 48 percent of the locations sampled, all ten drainages, and in nearly 90 percent of the ponds sampled. The pumpkinseed is distributed along Atlantic Slope drainages from New Brunswick to Georgia and west through the Great Lakes and upper Mississippi River drainages to Manitoba and Nebraska. It has now been widely introduced throughout North America.

Identification: Reaching a length of approximately 10.5 inches (267 mm), the body of this colorful species is generally olive or golden brown and covered with olive, orange, and rusty colored spots. There may be blue flecks on the sides of adults and blue wavy stripes that radiate from the mouth. The dorsal surface is darker then the ventral surface. Vertical bars or stripes are more noticeable on younger fish. The pumpkinseed is the only sunfish in Rhode Island with a red spot or margin on the opercular flap. Unlike the redbreast sunfish, the pectoral fins of the pumpkinseed are long and pointed, and when folded forward, extend beyond the eye.

Remarks: Pumpkinseeds are often referred to as "kivers" in some areas of New England. They are popular little pan fish that are easily caught in the shallow waters of a pond. Pumpkinseeds feed on a variety of aquatic insects, worms, snails, and crustaceans.

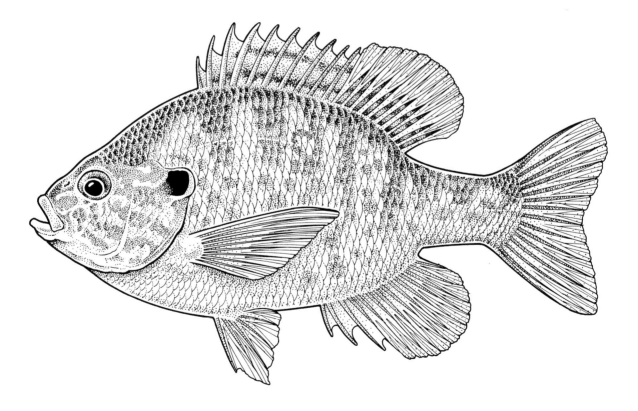

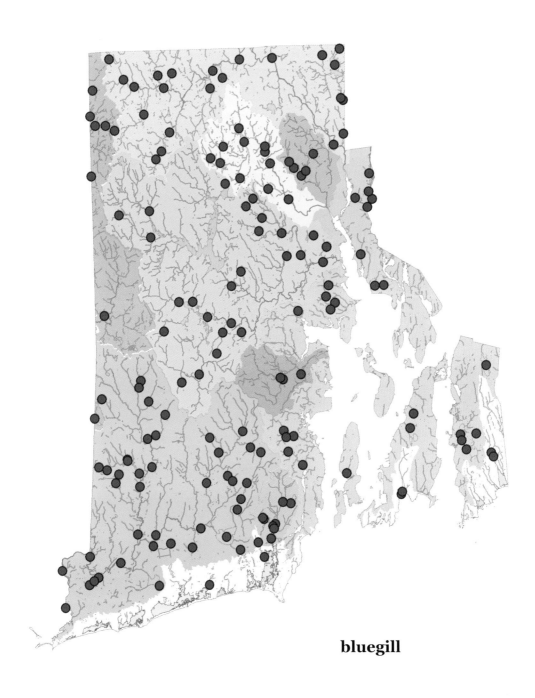

bluegill

bluegill
Lepomis macrochirus Rafinesque, 1819

Distribution: The bluegill was introduced into Rhode Island waters in 1914. It was the fourth most widely-distributed species collected and was found in more than 40 percent of the localities sampled, all ten drainages, and in more than 40 percent of the ponds sampled. The bluegill was formally distributed in the St. Lawrence, Great Lakes and Mississippi River basins from Minnesota east to western New York, and south to the Gulf of Mexico. It also occurs along Atlantic Slope drainages from Virginia to Florida and west to Texas. It is now widely distributed in North America, Europe, and South Africa. Bluegills were collected, for the most part, from lakes and ponds and from the sluggish areas of streams and rivers.

Identification: Bluegills as long as 9.5 inches (241 mm) were collected. The body of the bluegill is dark olive-green or olive-brown, becoming lighter lower on the sides. Dark vertical bands or stripes occur along its sides. The breast is a coppery-red in mature males and a lighter shade in females during the breeding season. Distinguishing features of this species are an opercular flap that is all black and a prominent dark blotch on the soft-rayed portion of the dorsal fin of older fish. The pectoral fins, similar to the pumpkinseed, are long and pointed and, when folded forward, extend beyond the eye.

Remarks: Bluegills feed on a variety of insects, small crustaceans, worms, and plant material.

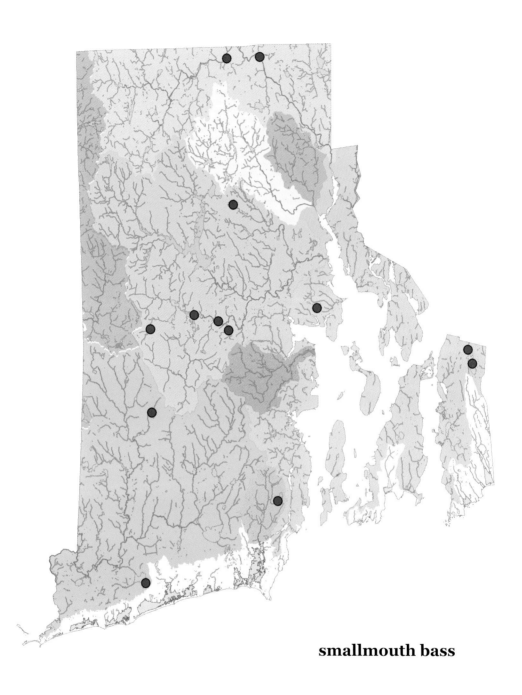

smallmouth bass

smallmouth bass
Micropterus dolomieu Lacepede, 1802

Distribution: The smallmouth bass is an important game fish that was first introduced in 1870. It was collected primarily from the rocky and gravelly areas of a few widely-dispersed ponds and streams. It is native to the upper Mississippi River, St. Lawrence, and Great Lakes basins, from Minnesota east to western New York and south to Oklahoma and Tennessee. However, it is now widely distributed in North America and elsewhere in the world.

Identification: Smallmouth bass as long as 17 inches (432 mm) were collected. The body of the smallmouth bass is brown or bronze in color with distinctive vertical bars. The eyes are usually orange or red; dark bars radiate from around the eyes. The length of the upper jaw, which extends to just below the middle of the eye, distinguishes this species from the largemouth bass, whose upper jaw extends beyond the eye. Young smallmouth bass lack the mid-lateral band common on juvenile largemouth bass. The tail of young smallmouth bass is tri-colored, having an orange base, a black band, and white tips.

Remarks: The smallmouth bass and largemouth bass, collectively referred to as black bass, are large carnivores at the top of the food chain that feed on a variety of animals, including fish, small mammals, frogs, and crayfish. Black bass are the most sought-after freshwater game fish in Rhode Island.

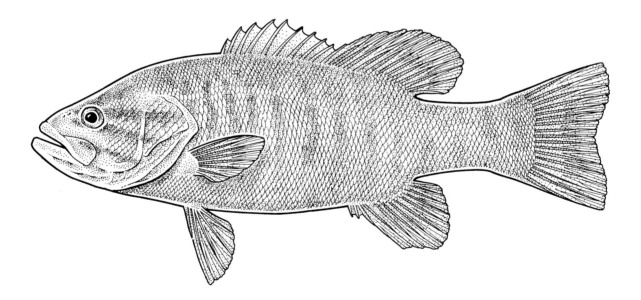

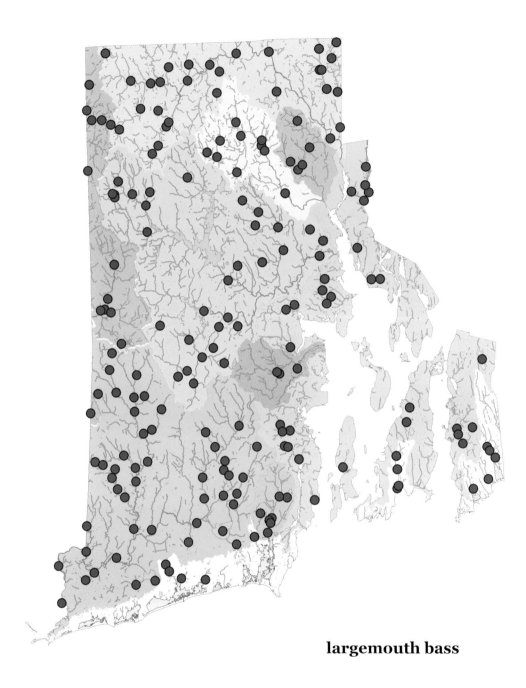

largemouth bass

largemouth bass
Micropterus salmoides (Lacepede, 1802)

Distribution: An important game fish that was introduced in 1896, the largemouth bass was the second most widely-distributed fish collected. It occurred in 51 percent of the localities sampled, all ten watersheds, and 95 percent of the lakes and ponds surveyed. Largemouth bass were originally distributed from the Great Lakes and St. Lawrence basins, south to Florida, Texas, and northern Mexico, and along the Atlantic slope drainages from North Carolina to Florida. However, it has been widely introduced elsewhere.

Identification: One of the largest bass collected was nearly 22 inches (559 mm) long and weighed more than 6 pounds (2.7 kg). The dorsal surface is dark green, appearing almost black, becoming lighter ventrally. A prominent dark lateral band is almost always apparent. Young bass also have a dark lateral band and a bi-colored tail. The length of the upper jaw is a characteristic commonly used to distinguish this species from the smallmouth bass. Unlike the smallmouth bass, whose upper jaw extends to just below the middle of the eye, the jaw of the largemouth bass extends beyond the eye.

Remarks: The largemouth bass and smallmouth bass, collectively referred to as black bass, are large carnivores at the top of the food chain that feed on a variety of animals, including fish, small mammals, frogs, and crayfish. Black bass are the most sought after freshwater game fish in Rhode Island.

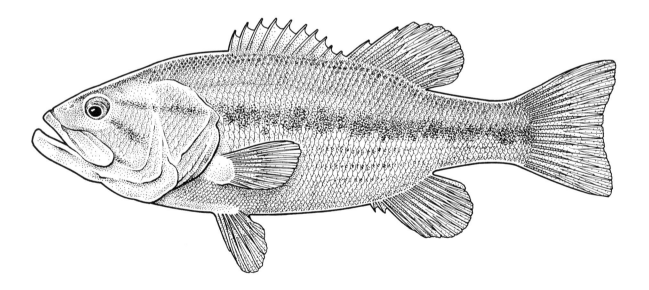

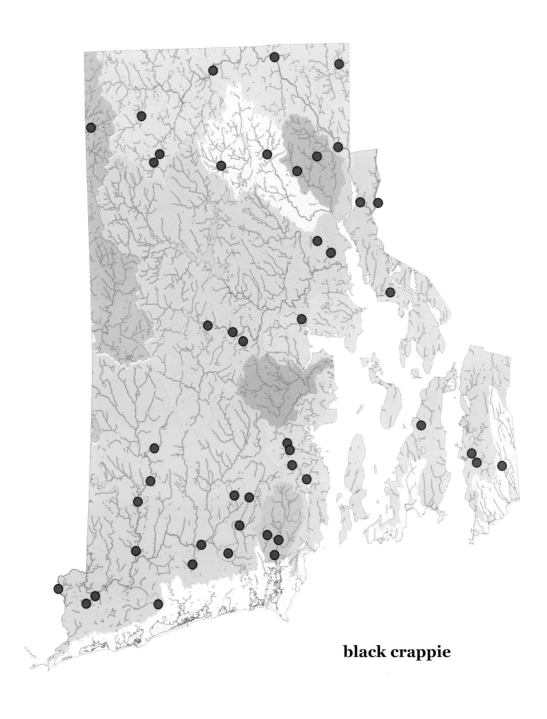

black crappie

black crappie
Pomoxis nigromaculatus (Lesueur, 1829)

Distribution: The black crappie is an introduced species that was collected from a few widely-dispersed locations throughout the state in both streams and ponds. The geographic distribution of black crappie is similar to that of the largemouth and smallmouth bass. Originally, black crappie were found from the St. Lawrence and Great Lakes basins, south to Texas and Florida, the Appalachians west to the Dakotas and Oklahoma, and Atlantic slope drainages from Virginia to Florida. Like the largemouth and smallmouth bass, it has been widely introduced in North America and throughout the world.

Identification: Black crappies as long as 13 inches (330 mm) were collected. The body of this fish is deep and laterally compressed. Its dorsal surface is dark green to almost black, and its sides are silvery-green and covered with small irregular dark blotches. The dorsal, caudal, and anal fins are dark and covered with light spots.

Remarks: The current Rhode Island sportfishing record for the black crappie is 15 inches (381 mm), 3 pounds (1.4 kg). They feed on a variety of invertebrates and small fish.

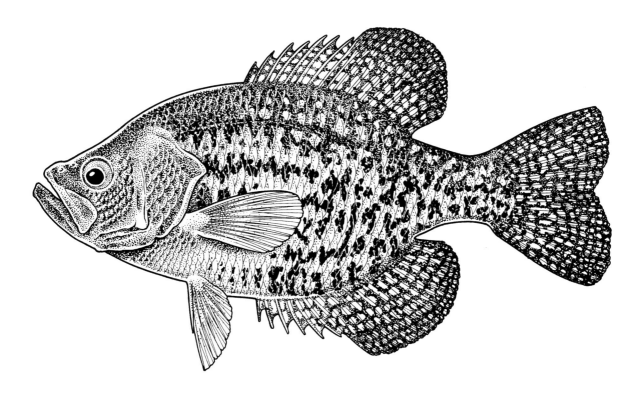

Perches
Family Percidae

This family is found in the cold and temperate freshwaters of the Northern Hemisphere. Of the 188 species found in North America, three were collected during this survey. Percids are the second largest family in North America, after cyprinids. Most species are small, less than 4 inches (102 mm) in length. They are slender, somewhat laterally compressed, and possess two separate dorsal fins, the first with spines and the second with rays.

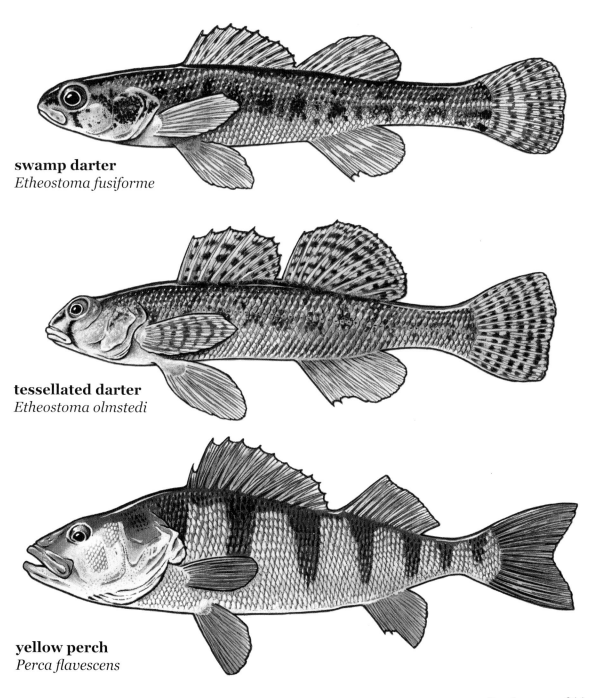

swamp darter
Etheostoma fusiforme

tessellated darter
Etheostoma olmstedi

yellow perch
Perca flavescens

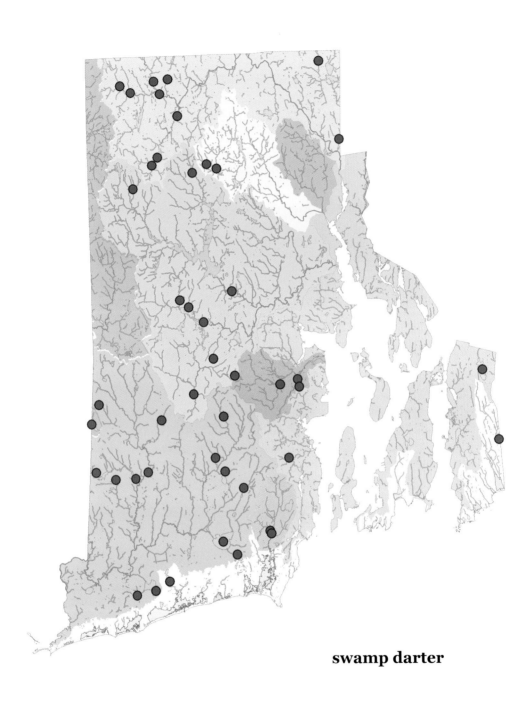

swamp darter

swamp darter
Etheostoma fusiforme (Girard, 1854)

Distribution: This small native species was collected throughout the state from a greater proportion of lakes and ponds than streams. Swamp darters are demersal and typically found in the still and slow-flowing waters of Atlantic Slope drainages from Maine to Florida and west along the Gulf Slope drainages to Texas.

Identification: The swamp darter, reaching 2.25 inches (57 mm) in length, is generally dark reddish brown in color. The lateral line, which arches towards the first dorsal fin, distinguishes this fish from the larger tessellated darter.

Remarks: This short-lived fish, rarely surviving beyond its second summer, feeds on small crustaceans and a variety of small aquatic insect larvae.

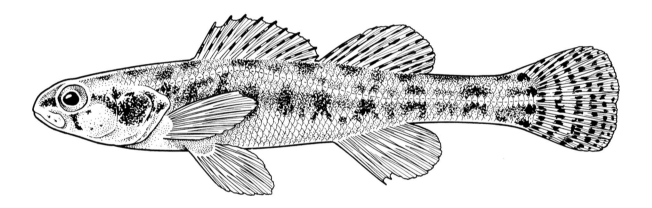

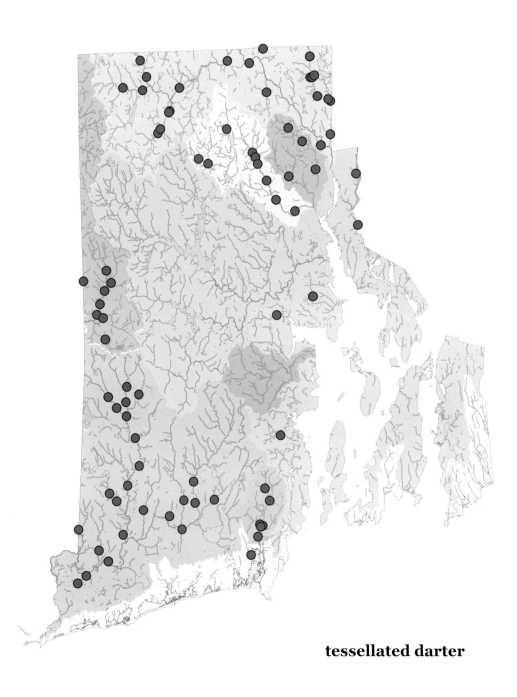

tessellated darter

tessellated darter
Etheostoma olmstedi Storer, 1842

Distribution: The tessellated darter is a small, native freshwater fish that was the eleventh most widely-distributed species collected. It occurred in more than 20 percent of locations sampled, eight drainages, and in a greater proportion of streams than ponds. Specimens were collected from all but the Pawtuxet and Hunt River watersheds. Tessellated darters are found primarily in streams from Quebec south along Atlantic slope drainages from New Hampshire to Florida.

Identification: Tessellated darters as long as 3.75 inches (95 mm) were collected. The body of the tessellated darter is generally gray-brown, becoming lighter below. The sides are covered with a series of dark X and W-shaped marks. A relatively flat lateral line distinguishes this species from the swamp darter.

Remarks: The diet of tessellated darters consists of small crustaceans and a variety of small aquatic insect larvae.

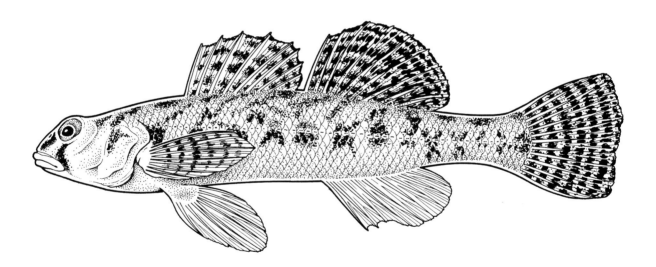

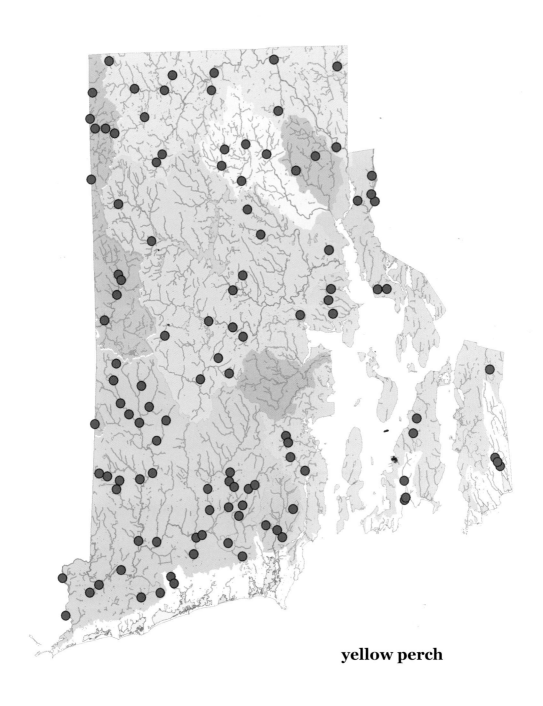

yellow perch

yellow perch
Perca flavescens (Mitchill, 1814)

Distribution: This native freshwater fish was the tenth most widespread species collected. It occurred in 30 percent of the localities sampled, nine of the ten drainages, and in a greater proportion of ponds than streams. Yellow perch were collected in all but the Hunt River watershed. In comparison to the swamp and tessellated darters, this relatively large fish is found in a variety of habitats that include warm and coldwater habitats from Nova Scotia to South Carolina and west to Missouri and Canada's Northwest Territories.

Identification: Yellow perch as long as 13 inches (330 mm) were collected. The body of the yellow perch is generally yellow-green in color with several dark green vertical bars that extend down from a dark green back. The lower fins are generally orange in color.

Remarks: The diet of the yellow perch, which changes with size and season, consists of aquatic invertebrates, fish eggs, and small fish. Young yellow perch, in turn, are preyed upon by many other species of fish, including bass and sunfish.

Bluefishes
Family Pomatomidae

This family, consisting of only a single species, is distributed around the world in tropical and subtropical marine waters. The bluefish is characterized by two dorsal fins (the first dorsal fin consists of a number of short spines and the second, and more conspicuous, consists of longer soft rays), a deeply forked tail, and a large head with sharp teeth.

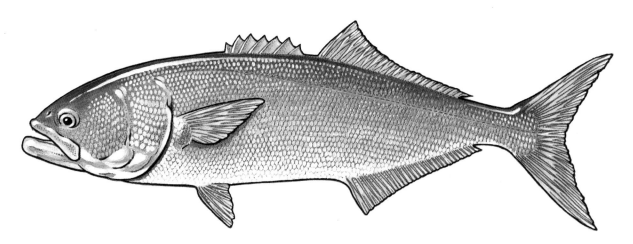

bluefish
Pomatomus saltatrix

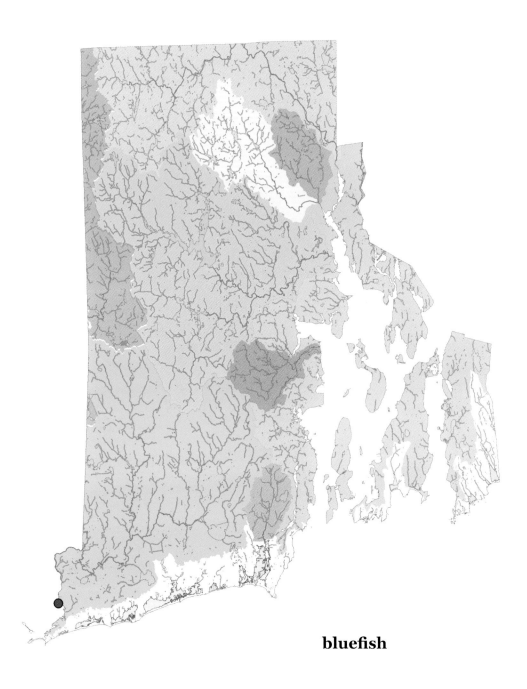

bluefish

bluefish
Pomatomus saltatrix (Linnaeus, 1766)

Distribution: Juveniles, 6 to 8 inches (152 – 203 mm) in length, are infrequently collected in the brackish waters of the lower Pawcatuck River. In the western Atlantic, the bluefish is found in offshore and inshore waters from Maine to Argentina. During the summer this important game fish may stray as far north as Nova Scotia.

Identification: Bluefish, which may reach a length of more than 40 inches (102 cm), are blue-green dorsally, becoming silvery along the sides and white ventrally. A large conspicuous head is armed with sharp teeth. The second dorsal fin and anal fin have distinctively long bases.

Remarks: This carnivore feeds voraciously, often killing more fish than it can consume. Bluefish are an important recreational species whose stocks were severely depleted from overfishing. Harvest restrictions have helped to rebuild numbers.

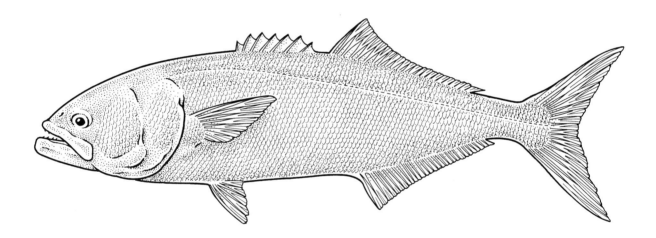

Jacks
Family Carangidae

This family is distributed worldwide, typically occurring in warm marine habitats. Fifty-five species are found in North America. Body shape in this family is extremely variable; many are deep and laterally compressed with a deeply-forked caudal fin. Many species are targeted by commercial and sport fishers.

crevalle jack
Caranx hippos
Juvenile

lookdown
Selene vomer
Juvenile

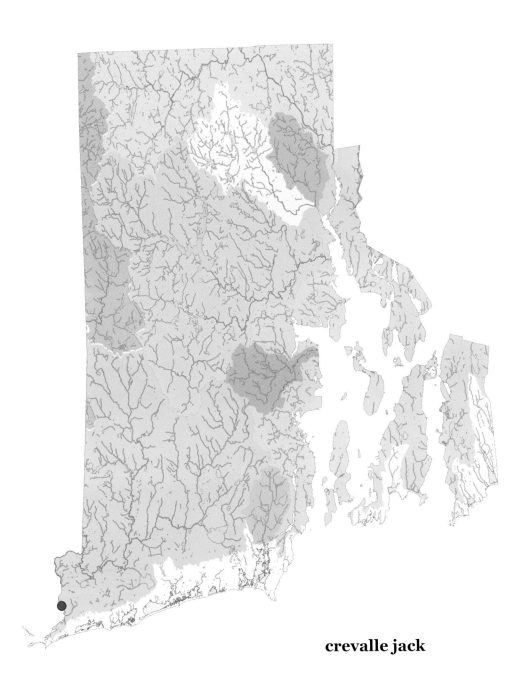

crevalle jack

crevalle jack
Caranx hippos (Linnaeus, 1766)

Distribution: Juveniles, approximately 1.5 to 3 inches (40 – 76 mm) long, are occasionally collected in the brackish water of the lower Pawcatuck River. Crevalle jacks are found offshore and in inshore waters from Nova Scotia to Uruguay.

Identification: The body of this fish is deep and laterally compressed. The head is blunt with a distinct black spot on the opercle and the tail is distinctly forked. The color of this jack is variable and changes with age. Young jacks, approximately 1 inch (25.4 mm) long, have distinct yellow and black vertical bands, which tend to fade as the fish grows larger. Fish that are approximately 3 inches (76 mm) long become silvery in color with faint vertical bands; shades of yellow appear ventrally on the body and fins. Adult crevalle jacks are bluish-green above with silvery sides that may have yellowish blotches. This species is distinguished from the yellow jack (*Caranx bartholomaei*), a species that has been collected elsewhere in Rhode Island waters (Powell 2001), by black spots found on the opercles and on the scimitar-shaped pectoral fins, a small patch of scales between the pelvic fins and a maxillary that extends to almost below the posterior edge of the eye.

Remarks: Adults are important game fish in some areas and may reach a length of approximately 40 inches (102 cm). Crevalle jacks feed on a variety of invertebrates and fish.

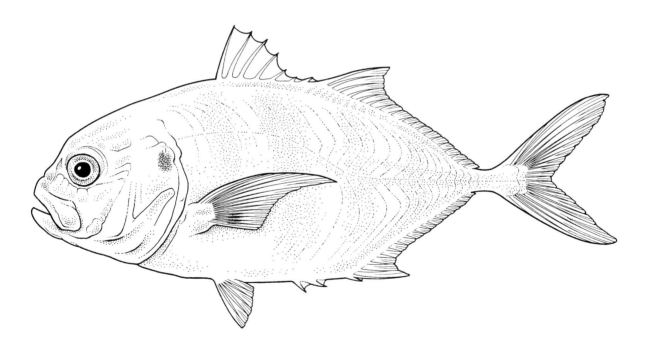

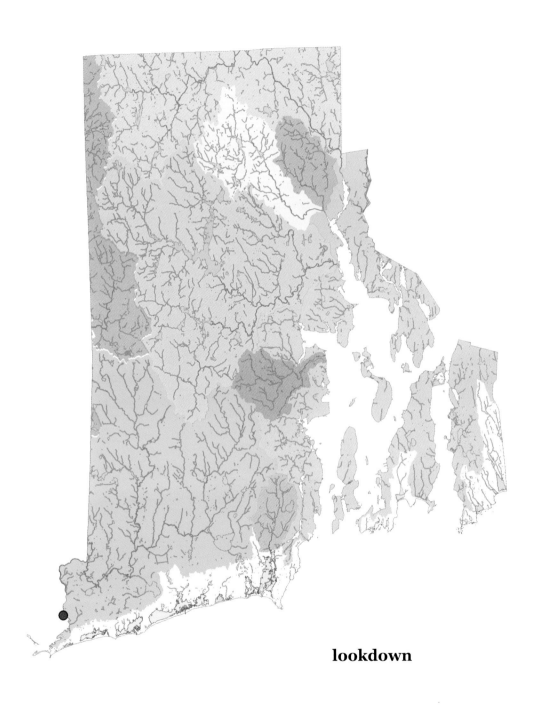

lookdown

lookdown
Selene vomer (Linnaeus, 1758)

Distribution: Young lookdowns, approximately 2 inches (51 mm) in length, are occasionally collected during the fall in the brackish water of the lower Pawcatuck River. Lookdowns are found in coastal waters of the western Atlantic from Maine to Uruguay.

Identification: The body of the lookdown is very deep and extremely compressed (laterally). The eyes are set high and the mouth low on a silvery body. The first few rays of the first dorsal and pelvic fins are extremely long and filamentous on juveniles and the body is silvery with several dusky yellow blotches or bars. As the fish grows these fin rays become shorter. A distinguishing feature that now becomes apparent are the elongated rays of the anterior portions of the second dorsal fin and the anal fin. Adults may reach lengths of 12 to 16 inches (305 - 406 mm).

Remarks: This small carnivore feeds on a variety of small worms, fish, and crustaceans.

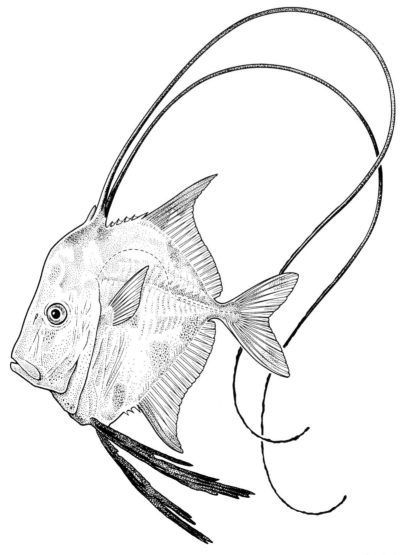

Snappers
Family Lutjanidae

This family is mainly marine and is found in tropical and subtropical waters of the Atlantic, Pacific, and Indian Oceans. Twenty-eight species of snappers are found in North America. Family members are generally characterized by somewhat deep and moderately compressed bodies. They have dorsal fins that are continuous or slightly notched and contain both spines and soft rays. They also have relatively large mouths containing enlarged canine teeth.

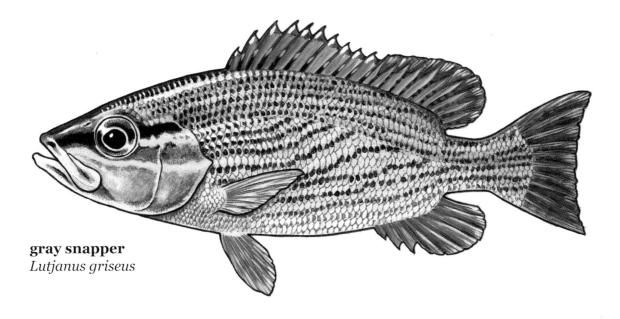

gray snapper
Lutjanus griseus

gray snapper

gray snapper
Lutjanus griseus (Linnaeus, 1758)

Distribution: Found in coastal waters of the western Atlantic from Massachusetts to Rio de Janeiro, juvenile gray snappers are occasionally collected in the fall in the brackish waters of the lower Pawcatuck River.

Identification: Young gray snappers, approximately 2 inches (51 mm) in length, are characterized by a prominent dark stripe that passes through the eye and a blue stripe below the eye. There are rows of small reddish-brown or orange spots on the sides of young fish. The blue stripe below the eye tends to fade as the fish matures. Adults may reach a length of 18 to 24 inches (457 – 610 mm).

Remarks: This important recreational species feeds on a variety of small fish and crustaceans.

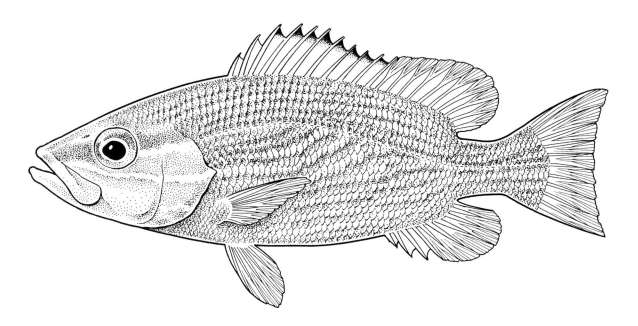

Mojarras
Family Gerreidae

This family consists of 40 species and is distributed worldwide, typically in tropical waters. Twenty-two species are found in North America. Fish in this family tend to be small and silvery. Bodies tend to be moderately deep to slender and laterally compressed; the caudal fins are deeply forked.

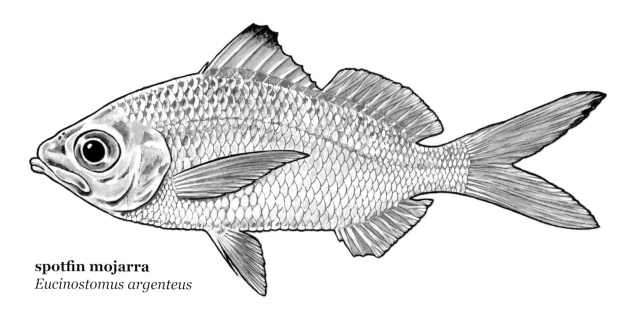

spotfin mojarra
Eucinostomus argenteus

spotfin mojarra

spotfin mojarra
Eucinostomus argenteus (Baird & Girard, 1855)

Distribution: The spotfin mojarra is generally found in the coastal waters of the western Atlantic from New Jersey to Brazil, including Bermuda, the Gulf of Mexico, and the Caribbean. Young spotfin mojarra are infrequently collected in the brackish waters of the lower Pawcatuck River and have been collected elsewhere in Rhode Island's coastal waters (Satchwill 2003).

Identification: Young spotfin mojarra, approximately 2 to 3 inches (51 – 76 mm) long, are silvery in color, laterally compressed, and possess a deeply forked caudal fin. The dark tip of the first dorsal fin is characteristic of this species. Adults are also silvery and may reach a length of approximately 8 inches (203 mm).

Remarks: These inshore fishes, generally found over soft bottoms, have extremely protrusible mouths, enabling them to feed on benthic invertebrates.

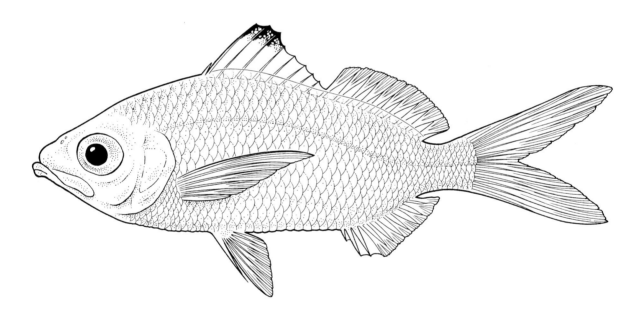

Wrasses
Family Labridae

More than 500 species are distributed worldwide in temperate and tropical waters. The size of wrasses is variable, ranging from more than 7 feet (2 m) to less than 6 inches (15 cm) in length. However, the majority of species are less than 12 inches (300 mm) in length. Many are very colorful and can change color and sex with growth. The smaller varieties are popular aquarium fishes. Wrasses are characteristized by long dorsal fins that extend from the head to the caudal peduncle. Among the 42 species that occur in North America, one was collected.

tautog
Tautoga onitis

tautog

tautog
Tautoga onitis (Linnaeus, 1758)

Distribution: Young fish, approximately 2.25 inches (57 mm) long, are infrequently caught in the brackish water of the Pawcatuck River. The tautog, also known as blackfish, is found in the western Atlantic from Nova Scotia south to South Carolina in association with rocky shorelines, jetties, and pilings. They do not undergo long seasonal migrations but tend to move offshore as the water cools and inshore when it warms.

Identification: This robust fish, which may reach a length of approximately 3 feet (91 cm), is characterized by a blunt, rounded head with thick lips. Tautog have a single dorsal fin that is long and continuous, reaching from the head to the caudal peduncle, and a caudal fin that is somewhat rounded. Tautog coloration is variable, ranging from a dark olive-green or brown to a dull blackish or gray color. Mature males are generally dull black or gray in color dorsally and along their sides, and white below. A white chin is characteristic of a mature male. Adult females and the young are a mottled olive-green or brown on a lighter colored background.

Remarks: The tautog is a tasty game fish that feeds on crabs, clams, and mussels growing on rocky shorelines, reefs, and pilings. The catch of this popular recreational and commercial species is regulated to reduce fishing mortality. The state record is a 21 pound, 4 ounce specimen caught in 1954.

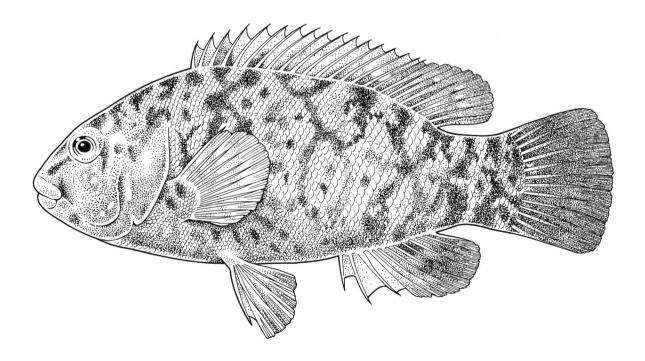

Porgies
Family Sparidae

Eighteen of these inshore warm water species are found in North America. However, only one species was collected during the survey. Species in this family are characteristized by deep and laterally compressed bodies, continuous dorsal fins with well-developed spiny and soft rays, forked caudal fins, and long pectoral fins.

pinfish
Lagodon rhomboides

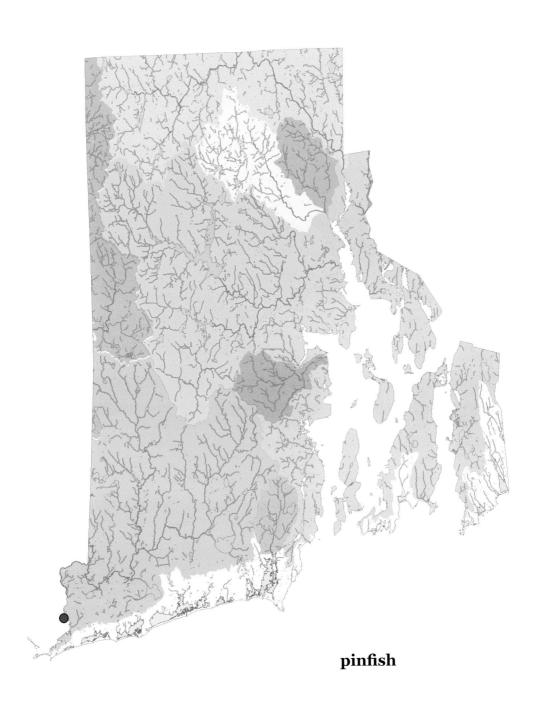

pinfish

pinfish
Lagodon rhomboides (Linnaeus, 1766)

Distribution: Pinfish are found from Cape Cod south to Mexico. Juveniles, 4 to 5 inches (102 – 127 mm) in length, are infrequently collected in the brackish waters of the lower Pawcatuck River in the fall.

Identification: Pinfish seldom exceed 8 inches (203 mm) in length and are bluish-silver with yellow horizontal stripes along the sides. The fins are yellowish and there is a distinctive black spot located behind the operculum. A few dusky vertical bars can also be noted along its sides.

Remarks: This carnivore feeds on a variety of marine invertebrates. Because of its hardiness, the pinfish is popular with anglers as a baitfish.

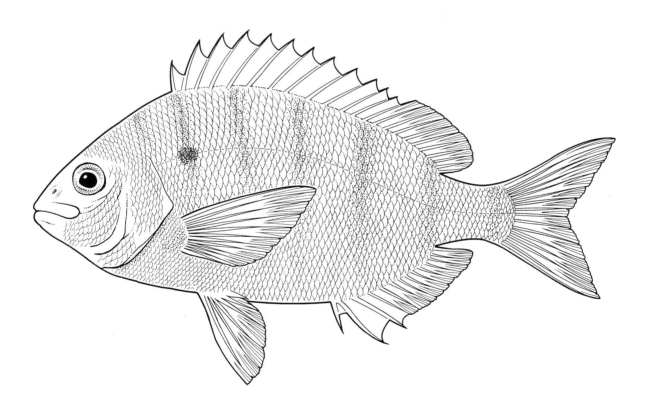

Drums
Family Sciaenidae

This large family, which is mostly marine, is widely distributed in the warm waters of North and South America and Asia. Among the eighty species that are found in North America, only two were collected during the survey. Drums are characteristized by two dorsal fins separated by a deep notch, caudal fins that vary from slightly concave to rounded, and elongate and moderately compressed bodies. Most are able to produce a noise that sounds like drumming.

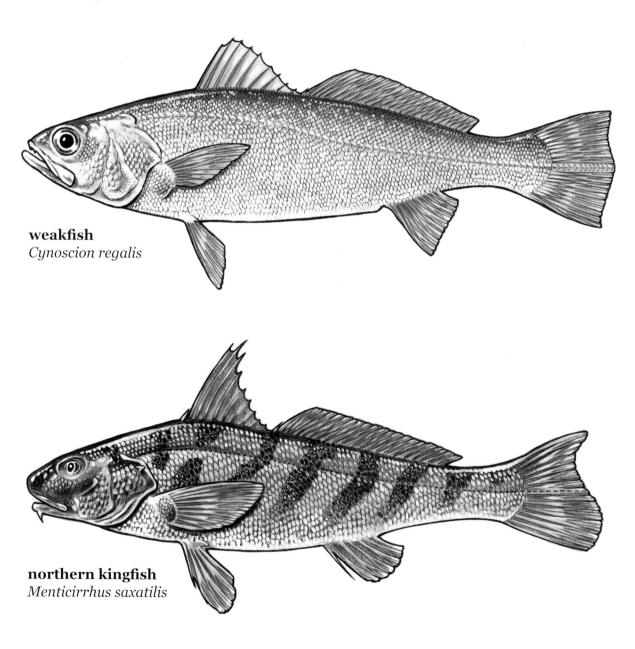

weakfish
Cynoscion regalis

northern kingfish
Menticirrhus saxatilis

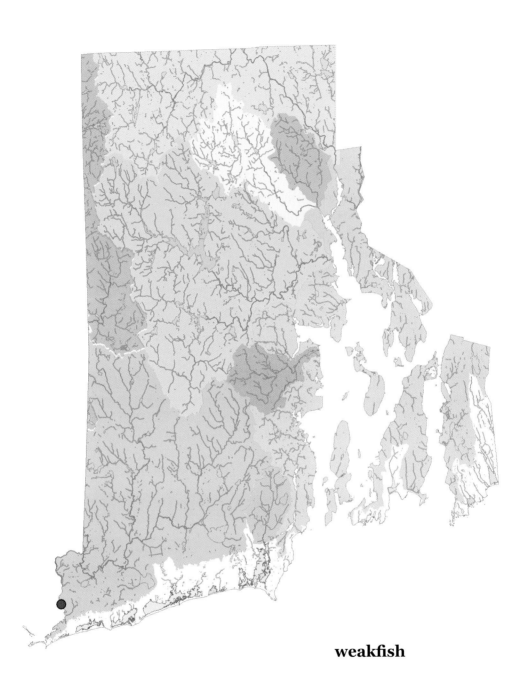

weakfish

weakfish
Cynoscion regalis (Bloch & Schneider, 1801)

Distribution: Juveniles, approximately 4 to 5 inches (102 – 127 mm) in length, are occasionally collected in the brackish waters of the lower Pawcatuck River. Young weakfish utilize estuaries as nursery areas in the warmer months of the year, then move offshore and south when the water cools. In North America the weakfish ranges along the Atlantic Coast from Nova Scotia to Florida.

Identification: Weakfish may reach a length of 30 to 36 inches (762 – 914 mm). As with most fish, color can vary according to surroundings. A weakfish is dark olive to bluish-green dorsally and silvery below. An iridescent blue, green, purple, or pink sheen may be noted along its sides. The body generally has an overall coppery or brassy cast. As it matures, spots begin to appear on the body. The fins of the weakfish are generally tinged in yellow. The caudal fin on young fish is rounded and as they mature the fin becomes indented or concave (emarginate). Unlike the northern kingfish, the lower jaw of the weakfish projects beyond the upper jaw.

Remarks: This important recreational and commercial species is carnivorous, feeding primarily on shrimp and fish. Harvest regulations have been implemented in an attempt to reduce a decline in abundance.

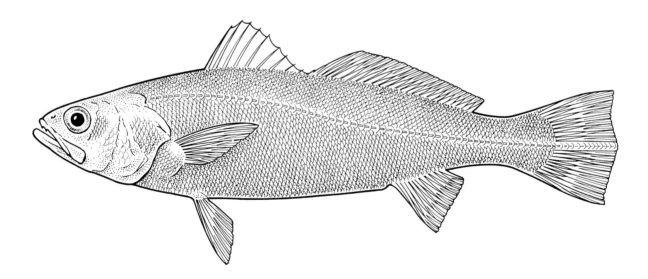

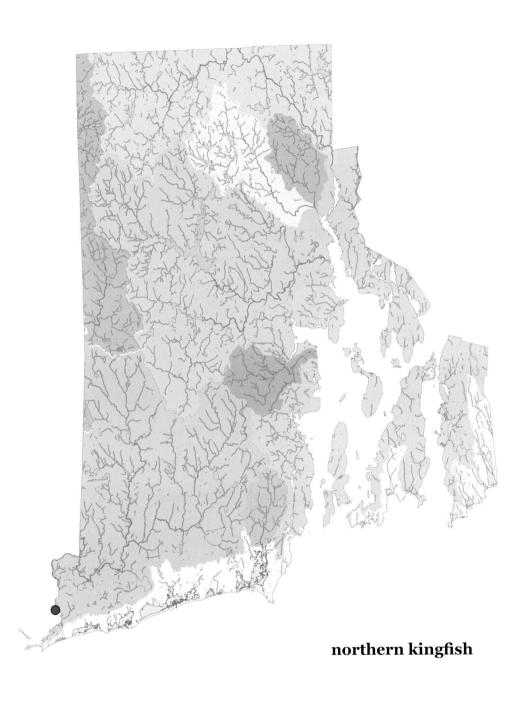

northern kingfish

northern kingfish
Menticirrhus saxatilis (Bloch & Schneider, 1801)

Distribution: Northern kingfish are distributed along the Atlantic Coast from Maine to Florida and into the Gulf of Mexico to Yucatan. Juveniles, 3 to 4 inches (76 –102 mm) long, are occasionally collected in the fall in the brackish waters of the lower Pawcatuck River.

Identification: Kingfish may reach a length of 17 inches (432 mm). They are dusky above and whitish below with dark, almost black, diagonal bars along the sides. A long spine on the first dorsal fin, an overhanging upper jaw, and a single chin barbel distinguish this species from the weakfish.

Remarks: This fish, popular with many saltwater anglers, is a carnivore feeding on a variety of organisms.

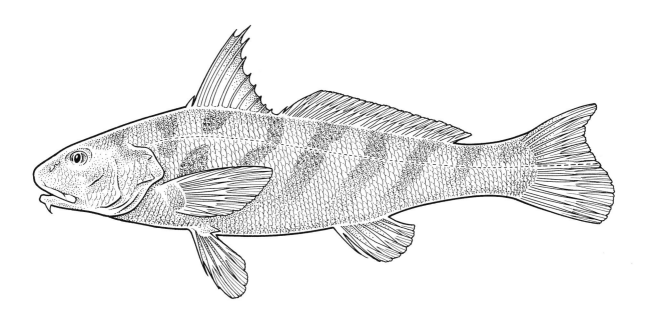

Gobies
Family Gobiidae

 This large family consists of more than 1,500 species and is found worldwide in coastal tropical (mostly) and temperate waters. Of the 136 species found in North America, one was collected. The pelvic fins of these generally small fish are usually modified to form a suction disk, by which it can attach itself to rocks in moving water.

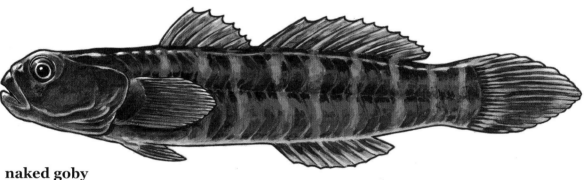

naked goby
Gobiosoma bosc

naked goby

naked goby
Gobiosoma bosc (Lacepede, 1800)

Distribution: Naked gobies, found along the Atlantic Coast from Massachusetts to Florida, are occasionally collected in the brackish waters of the lower Pawcatuck River.

Identification: This small, scaleless fish rarely exceeds 3 inches (76 mm) in length. It is greenish or dusky brown in color dorsally, becoming pale below. Light vertical bars occur along its sides. Pelvic fins are modified to form a suction disk that it uses to cling to rocks and aquatic weeds.

Remarks: Gobies are bottom-dwelling carnivores. They feed on small fish, crustaceans, worms, etc. that pass by the rocks or shells they use for shelter. In turn, gobies are preyed upon by many other larger fish.

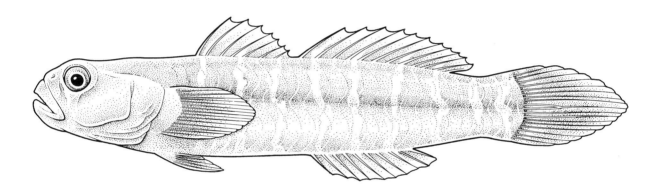

Butterfishes
Family Stromateidae

This family is found worldwide in temperate and tropical waters. Of the seven species found in North America, one was collected. Species in this family are characterized by deep, laterally compressed bodies.

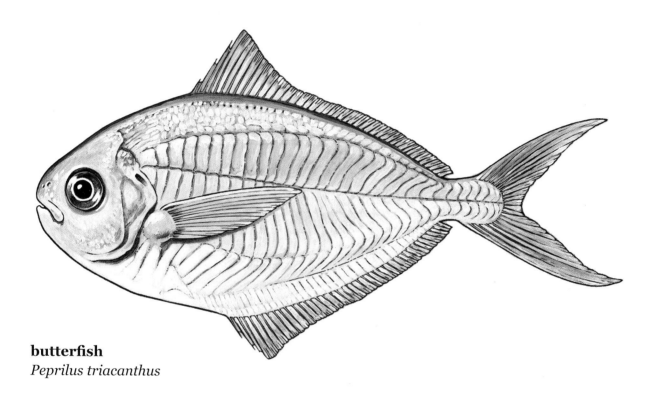

butterfish
Peprilus triacanthus

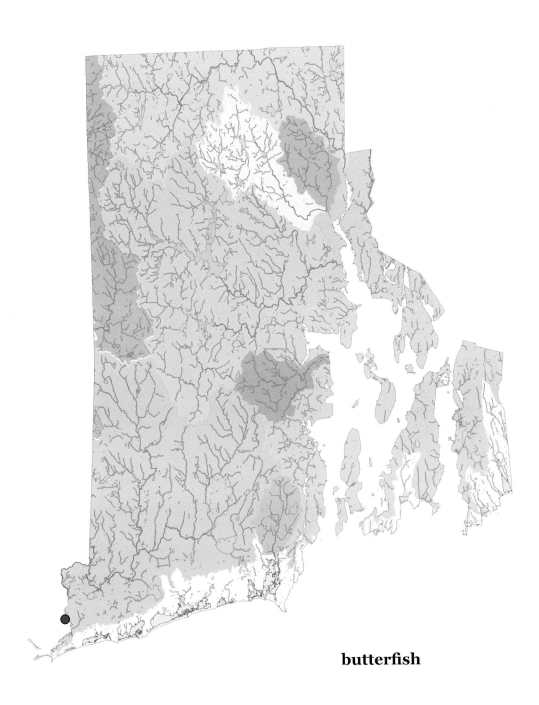

butterfish

butterfish
Peprilus triacanthus (Peck, 1804)

Distribution: The young of this species are occasionally collected in the brackish waters of the lower Pawcatuck River. As the water cools, butterfish migrate offshore or down the coast. They are distributed along the Atlantic Coast from Newfoundland and the Gulf of St. Lawrence south to Florida and the Gulf of Mexico.

Identification: Although these fish can reach a length of 10 inches (254 mm), only young fish, approximately 1.5 inches (38 mm), were collected. The bodies of these silvery fish are deep, highly compressed, and almost oval in shape. The absence of pelvic fins is distinctive of this species. The pectoral fins are long and the caudal fin is deeply forked. The bases of the dorsal and anal fins are relatively long and continuous. The most anterior rays of these fins are longest. A number of large pores are found between the dorsal fin and lateral line. Scales are tiny and easily sloughed off.

Remarks: Butterfish feed on small fish, squid, and crustaceans and, in turn, are preyed upon by larger fish, including bluefish and swordfish. Young fish may often be seen swimming among the tentacles of large jellyfish to avoid predators. Landings of this commercially important fish have declined since the 1970s.

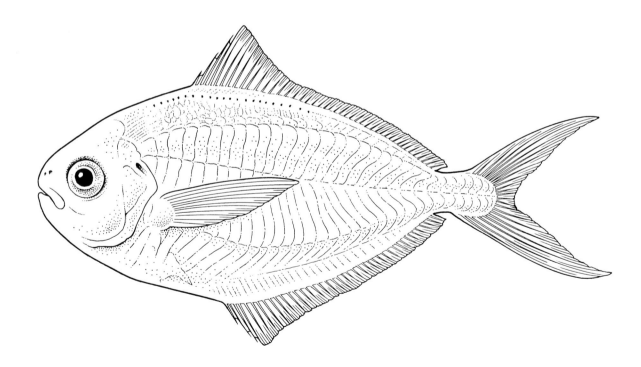

Turbots
Family Scophthalmidae

This family consists of only a single species and is found in the marine and brackish waters of North America and Europe. Both eyes are found on the left side of a deep and highly compressed (laterally) body. Like all flat fish, the young are born symmetrical with eyes on both sides of its body. However, during growth the right eye of turbots migrates to the left side and the fish begins swimming on its side.

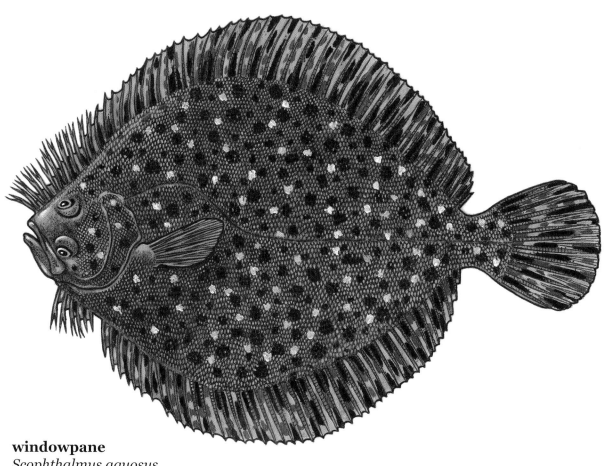

windowpane
Scophthalmus aquosus

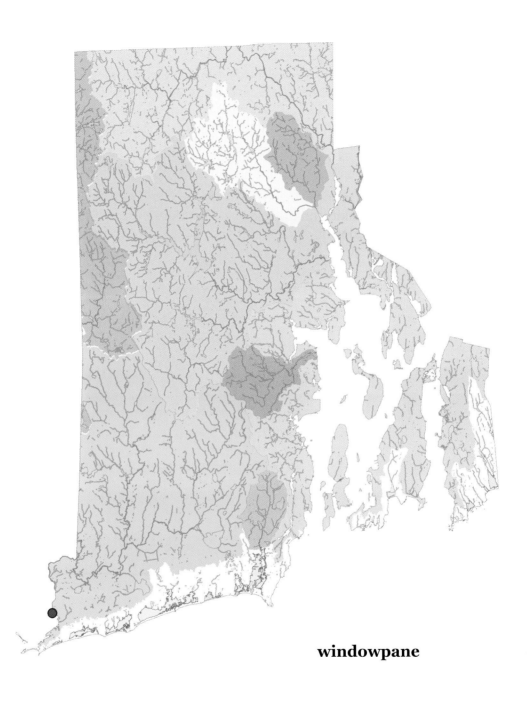

windowpane

windowpane
Scophthalmus aquosus (Mitchill, 1815)

Distribution: Juvenile windowpanes were collected in the brackish water of the lower Pawcatuck River. This species is distributed along the Atlantic Coast from the Gulf of St. Lawrence to South Carolina. Windowpane do not appear to undertake seasonal migrations like many other fish species. They can be found in Narragansett Bay throughout the year. Its preferred habitat consists of sandy and muddy bottoms in shallow water.

Identification: Windowpane may reach a length of approximately 18 inches (457 mm). The body of this left-eyed flatfish is rounded and relatively thin in comparison to most flounders. Color is variable, taking on the hue of the bottom substrate. The upper side is sometimes brown and covered with many darker brown spots. Also characteristic of this flounder is a relatively large mouth that lacks teeth and a highly arched lateral line.

Remarks: The population of this commercially and recreationally important species has declined in Narragansett Bay (DFW 2004). This carnivore feeds on a variety of crustaceans and small fish.

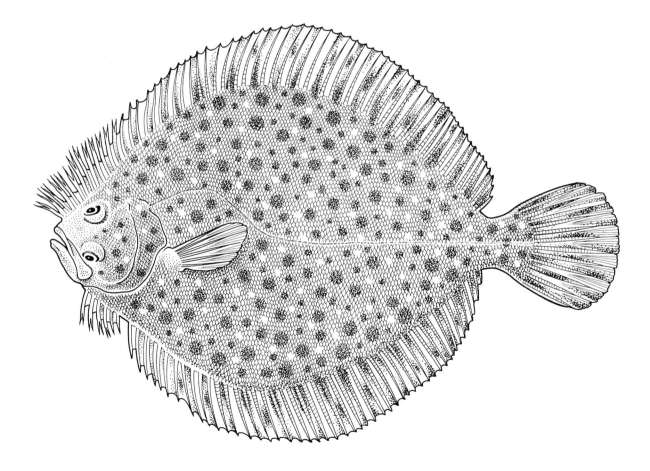

Righteye Flounders
Family Pleuronectidae

This family is benthic and found worldwide. Of 34 species found in North America, one was collected. Both eyes of this principally marine family are found on the right side of a deep and highly compressed (laterally) body. Like all flat fish, the young are born symmetrical with eyes on both sides of the body. The dorsal and anal fins are long and continuous. Many species are of commercial importance.

winter flounder
Pseudopleuronectes americanus

winter flounder

winter flounder
Pseudopleuronectes americanus (Walbaum, 1792)

Distribution: Juveniles, approximately 1.5 to 4 inches (38 – 102 mm) in length, were collected in the brackish water of the lower Pawcatuck River. Winter flounder occur along the Atlantic Coast from Labrador to Georgia, where they are generally found in coastal areas and estuaries with soft muddy bottoms.

Identification: The winter flounder is a right-eyed flatfish that may reach a length of 23 inches (584 mm). Color of the winter flounder varies a great deal and in many cases is a blotchy brown or olive. Like other flounders, they take on the hue of the bottom substrate. In contrast to the windowpane, the body of the winter flounder is oval-shaped and thicker, the mouth is small and contains teeth, and the lateral line is nearly straight.

Remarks: This once plentiful and commercially important fish, has been extensively over-fished, causing a substantial decline in stocks (DFW 2004). Harvest regulations and the identification of essential habitat have helped stocks to recover. Winter flounder feed on a wide variety of organisms that include crustaceans, worms, and molluscs.

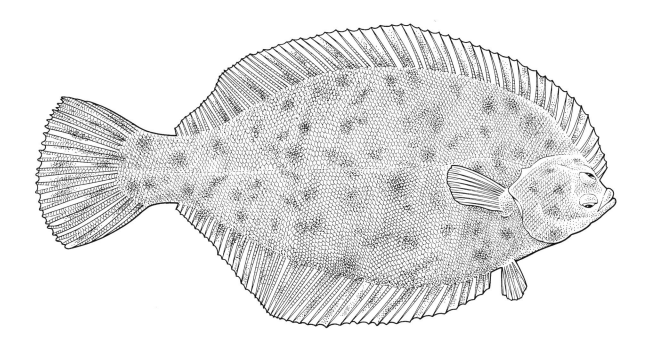

American Soles
Famliy Achiridae

Thirteen species of this mainly marine group of flatfish are found along the Atlantic and Pacific Coasts of North America. Members of this family are characterized by deep and highly compressed (laterally) bodies, two eyes that are located on the right side of the head, and the absence lack pectoral fins. The dorsal and anal fins are long and continuous. Like all flatfish, the young are born symmetrical with eyes located on each side of its body. However, during growth the left eye of American soles migrates to the right side and the fish begins swimming on its side. Only one species in this family was collected.

hogchoker
Trinectes maculatus

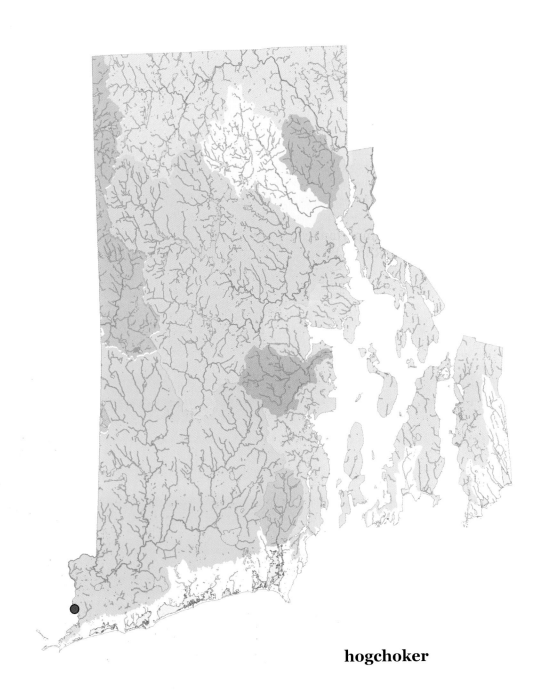

hogchoker

hogchoker
Trinectes maculatus (Bloch & Schneider, 1801)

Distribution: Juveniles, 1 to 2 inches (25 –51 mm) in length, of this small native flatfish were collected in the brackish water of the lower Pawcatuck River. The hogchoker is distributed in coastal waters along the Atlantic from Massachusetts to Panama.

Identification: The hogchoker seldom exceeds 8 inches (203 mm) in length. A distinguishing characteristic of this right-handed flatfish is the absence of pectoral fins. Depending on the substrate, its color ranges from a dusky brown to an olive brown above and pale below. The right side is often striped with light and dark bands.

Remarks: Although not an important commercial or recreational species, hogchoker populations are declining in Rhode Island (DFW 2004). This bottom-dwelling predator feeds on a variety of small invertebrates.

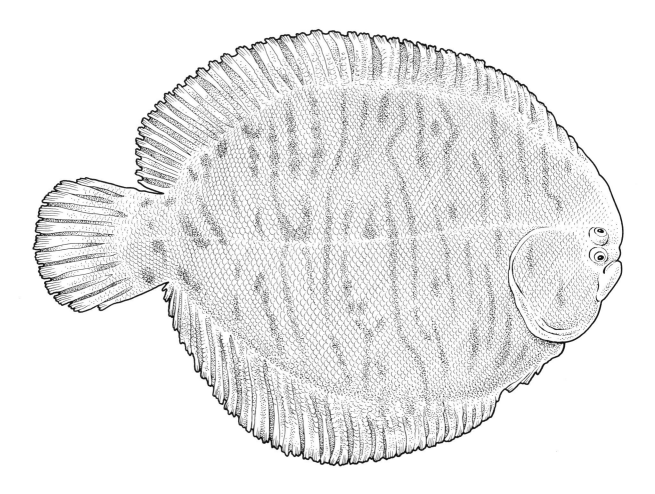

Glossary

Adipose fin – A small fleshy fin, lacking spines and rays, located on the dorsal surface between the dorsal and caudal fins.

Ammocoetes – The larval stage of a lamprey.

Anadromous – Fish that live in saltwater but spawn regularly in freshwater.

Anal fin – A fin located on the ventral surface between the caudal fin and anus.

Axillary process – A fleshy appendage or elongated scale that is located at the base of the pelvic fins of certain fish species.

Barbel – A slender fleshy appendage located near the mouth that contains sensory organs.

Benthic – Living on the bottom of a sea or lake.

Boney keel –Tissue or scales that form a sharp edge or ridge-like structure.

Carnivore – A flesh eating animal.

Cartilaginous – Refers to any structure that is based on cartilage.

Catadromous – Fish that live in freshwater but spawns regularly in saltwater.

Caudal fin – The tail fin of a fish.

Caudal peduncle – The structure that supports the tail fin.

Cheek – An area on the side of the head extending below and slightly behind the eye.

Cycloid Scale - A smooth rimed scale, characteristic of soft-rayed fish such as trouts and salmons or carps and minnows.

Diadromous - Fish that migrate regularly between freshwater and saltwater to spawn. See *anadromous* and *catadromous*.

Dorsal – The upper surface or back.

Dorsal fin – A fin or fins located on the upper surface of fishes or certain marine animals.

Endemic – Native to a certain region.

Filamentous – Threadlike.

Fishway (Fish ladder) – A device to assist migration that allows a fish passage around a barrier.

Flocculent – A substance having a fluffy character or appearance.

Frenum – A band of tissue that connects the upper lip to the snout.

Gill rakers – Projections along anterior edge of a gill arch that aid in food gathering.

Head-of-Tide – The furthest point upstream that is affected by the rise and fall of the tide.

Indigenous – A naturally occurring species.

Inferior Mouth – A mouth located distinctly behind an overhanging snout. See *oblique, subterminal* and *terminal mouth.*

Insertion – The anterior point of attachment or origin of the dorsal and anal fins.

Keel – A ridge-like structure.

Lateral line – A series of pores located along the sides of the body that contain sensory organs.

Lentic – Refers to standing water as in a pond.

Lotic – Refers to moving water as in a stream.

Maxillary – The posterior bone in the upper jaw.

Natal – Pertains to the time or place of birth.

Naturalized – A nonnative species that reproduces in the wild.

Nuptial Tubercles – Small rounded bumps that occur on the heads off some male species during the breeding season.

Oblique Mouth - The mouth, when closed, is angles at 45 degrees or more. See *inferior, subterminal* and *terminal mouth.*

Omnivore – An animal that feeds on both plant and animal matter.

Opercle – A large bone of the operculum or gill cover.

Operculum – Boney plates that cover a fish's gill, may also be referred to as a gill cover.

Opercular flap or ear flap – A small extension on the rear edge of the operculum.

Origin – Anterior-most point of attachment of dorsal or anal fins (i.e., insertion).

Papillae – Small fleshy protuberances found on the skin.

Parr marks – Dark bands or blotches located on the sides of some immature fish that usually disappears as the fish matures.

Pectoral fins – A pair of fins located posterior to the opercles (gill covers).

Pelagic – Pertains to the open sea or ocean.

Pelvic fins – A pair of fins located posterior to pectoral fins and on the ventral surface of the fish.

Peritoneum – The lining of the body cavity.

Pharyngeal teeth – Tooth-like structures on pharyngeal bones located behind the gill arches used for crushing food and also as an aid to identify fish.

Physiography – The study of the earth's land surfaces with emphasis on the origin and evolution of land forms.

Piscivorous – Feeding on fish.

Plankton – Small or microscopic plants (phytoplankton) or animals (zooplankton) that float or drift in the water column of fresh and saltwater.

Protractile (protrusible) – The ability to extend or thrust outward.

Ray – A flexible supporting structure in a fin that is segmented and is usually branched.

Refugia – Habitat that escaped change during adverse conditions.

Riffle – A shallow section of steam with choppy, fast flowing water.

Salinity - The contentration of salt and water usually expressed as parts-per-thousand (ppt).

Sargasso Sea – Part of the North Atlantic Ocean between the Azores and the West Indies.

Scimitar – A curved Oriental sword.

Snout length – The distance from the tip of the upper jaw to the front edge of the eye.

Spine – A stiff supporting structure in a fin that are typically not branched or segmented.

Standard length – Measured from the anterior most part of the head to the posterior margin of the boney plate which supports the rays of the caudal fin (hypural plate).

Stream order – A system used to classify streams that is based on the number of tributaries flowing into it from upstream areas and their branching patterns. The smallest unbranched stream with no tributaries is designated as a first (1) order stream and when joined with another first order stream becomes a second (2) order stream and so on.

Subterminal Mouth – Refers to a mouth that is located below and slightly behind the snout. See *inferior, oblique* and *terminal mouth*.

Terminal mouth – Refers to a mouth located at the tip of the snout where neither the upper or lower jaw project beyond the other. See *inferior, oblique* and *subterminal mouth*.

Total length - Measured from the anterior-most part of the head to the posterior-most part of the caudal fin.

Tubercles – Small rounded bumps that occur on the heads off some male species during the breeding season.

Wisconsinan Ice Age – The most recent period of the ice age that ended approximately 10,000 years ago in North America.

Zooplankton – See plankton.

Literature Cited

Army Corps of Engineers. 2001. Turner Reservoir Study, East Providence, RI. Section 22 Planning Assistance to States. January 2001, US Army Corps of Engineers, New England District.

Bigelow, H.B. and W.S. Schroeder. 1953. Fishes of the Gulf of Maine. Fishery Bulletin 74, Fishery bulletin of the Fish and Wildlife Service (Contribution No. 592, Woods Hole Oceanographic Institution). United States Government Printing Office, Washington. 577pp.

Boschung, Jr., H.T., J.D. Williams, D.W. Gotshall, D.K. Caldwell, and M.C. Caldwell. 1983. The Audubon Society Field Guide to North American Fishes, Whales, and Dolphins. Alfred A. Kopf, Inc. 848pp.

Buckley, B.B. and S.W. Nixon. 2001. An historical assessment of anadromous fish in the Blackstone River. University of Rhode island, Graduate School of Oceanography. 26pp.

CIF (Commissioners of Inland Fisheries). 1872. Second Annual Report made to the General Assembly at its January Session, 1872. A. Crawford Greene, Printer to the State, Providence, R.I.

CIF (Commissioners of Inland Fisheries). 1874. Fourth Annual Report made to the General Assembly at its January Session, 1874. Providence Press Company, Printers to the State, Providence, R.I.

CIF (Commissioners of Inland Fisheries). 1881. Tenth Annual Report made to the General Assembly at its January Session, 1881. E.L. Freeman & Company, Printers to the State, Providence, R.I.

CIF (Commissioners of Inland Fisheries). 1891. Annual Report made to the General Assembly at its January Session, 1891. E.L. Freeman & Company, Printers to the State, Providence, R.I.

CIF (Commissioners of Inland Fisheries). 1895. Annual Report made to the General Assembly at its January Session, 1895. E.L. Freeman & Company, Printers to the State, Providence, R.I.

CIF (Commissioners of Inland Fisheries). 1896. Annual Report made to the General Assembly at its January Session, 1896. E.L. Freeman & Company, Printers to the State, Providence, R.I.

CIF (Commissioners of Inland Fisheries). 1899. Twenty-ninth Annual Report made to the General Assembly at its January Session, 1899. E.L. Freeman & Sons, Providence, R.I.

CIF (Commissioners of Inland Fisheries). 1900. Thirtieth Annual Report made to the General Assembly at its January Session, 1900. E.L. Freeman & Sons, Providence, R.I.

CIF (Commissioners of Inland Fisheries). 1911. Forty-first Annual Report made to the General Assembly at its January Session, 1911. E.L. Freeman & Sons, Providence, R.I.

CIF (Commissioners of Inland Fisheries). 1915. Forty-fifth Annual Report made to the General Assembly at its January Session, 1915. E.L. Freeman & Sons, Providence, R.I.

CIF (Commissioners of Inland Fisheries). 1917. Forty-seventh Annual Report made to the General Assembly at its January Session, 1917. E.L. Freeman & Sons, Providence, R.I.

DA&C (Department of Agriculture and Conservation). 1939. Fifth Annual Report to the State of R.I. and Providence Plantations for the period January 1, 1939 to December 31, 1939.

DA&C (Department of Agriculture and Conservation). 1940. Sixth Annual Report to the State of R.I. and Providence Plantations for the period January 1, 1940 to December 31, 1940.

DA&C (Department of Agriculture and Conservation). 1953. Eighteenth Annual Report to the State of R.I. and Providence Plantations for the period July 1, 1952 to June 30, 1953.

Demaine, A.W. 1981. Hunt River watershed stream survey. Rhode Island Division of Fish and Wildlife Fisheries Report No. 7. Federal Aid to Fisheries Project, F-20-R. 18pp.

Demaine, A.W. and R.C. Guthrie. 1979. Blackstone River watershed stream survey. Rhode Island Division of Fish and Wildlife Fisheries Report No. 4. Federal Aid to Fisheries Project, F-20-R. 28pp.

Demaine, A.W. and J.F. O'Brien. 1980. Saugatucket River watershed stream survey. Rhode Island Division of Fish and Wildlife Fisheries Report No. 6. Federal Aid to Fisheries Project, F-20-R. 21pp.

DFW (Division of Fish & Wildlife). 2004. Rhode Island Fisheries Stock Status: an overview 2004. Report presented to the General Assembly by Division of Fish and Wildlife, Fort Wetherill Marine Laboratory, 3 Wetherill Road, Jamestown, RI 02835. 21 pp.

Edwards, P.A. and S.D. Olszewski. 1990. Landlocked alewife (*Alosa pseudoharengus*) investigations in Beach Pond, Stafford Pond, and Wallum Lake. Division of Fish and Wildlife, Rhode Island Department of Environmental Management, Federal Aid in Sport Fish Restoration Act F-20-R. Research Reference Document 90.2. 10 pp.

Everhart, W.H. 1976. Fishes of Maine. Maine Department of Inland Fisheries and Wildlife. 4th Edition. 96pp.

Fellows, N.W., Jr. 1940. Rhode Island stream survey. A general report of a stream survey of the trout waters of Rhode Island to Rhode Island Office of Fish and Game, H.N. Gibbs, Administrator.

Fenneman, N.M. 1938. Physiography of Eastern United States. McGraw-Hill Book Company, Inc, New York and London. 714pp.

Fuller, P.L., L.G. Nico, and J.D. Williams. 1999. Nonindigenous Fishes Introduced into Inland Waters of the United States. American Fisheries Society, Special Publication 27, Bethesda, Maryland. 613pp.

Guenther, C.B. and A. Spacie. 2006. Changes in Fish Assemblage Structure Upstream of Impoundments within the Upper Wabash River Basin, Indiana. Transactions of the American Fisheries Society 135:570-583.

Guthrie, R.C. 1980. Moosup River watershed stream survey. Rhode Island Division of Fish and Wildlife Fisheries Report No. 5. Federal Aid to Fisheries Project, F-20-R. 48pp.

Guthrie, R.C., J.A. Stolgitis, and W.L. Bridges. 1973. Pawcatuck River watershed: Fisheries management survey. Rhode Island Division of Fish and Wildlife Fisheries Report Number 1. Federal Aid to Fisheries Project, F-20-R. 59pp.

Guthrie, R.C. and J.A. Stolgitis. 1977. Fisheries investigations and management in Rhode Island lakes and ponds. Rhode Island Division of Fish and Wildlife Fisheries Report Number 3. Federal Aid to Fisheries Project, F-20-R. 256pp.

Hartel, K.E., D.B. Halliwell, and A.E. Launer. 2002. Inland Fishes of Massachusetts. Massachusetts Audubon Society. 328pp.

Jacobs, R.P. and E.B. O'Donnell. 2009. A Pictorial Guide to Freshwater Fishes of Connecticut. Connecticut Department of Environmental Protection, Bulletin 42. 242pp.

Jenkins, R.E. and N.M. Burkhead. 1993. Freshwater fishes of Virginia. American Fisheries Society, Bethesda, Maryland. 1078pp.

Kanehl, P.D., J.L. Lyons, and J.E. Nelson. 1997. Changes in the Habitat and Fish Community of the Milwaukee River, Wisconsin, following Removal of the Woolen Mill Dam. North American Journal of Fisheries Management 17:387-400.

Krueger, W.H. 2001. Freshwater Fishes. Pages 9-13. *in* P.V. August, R.W. Enser, and L.L. Gould, editors. Vertebrates of Rhode Island, Volume 2. The Biota of Rhode Island. Rhode Island Natural History Survey.

Langdon, R.W., M.T. Ferguson, and K.M. Cox. 2006. Fishes of Vermont. Published by the Vermont Department of Fish and Wildlife, Waterbury, Vermont. 320pp.

Lapin, W.J. 1992. Lake Management. Performance Report. Rhode Island Department of Environmental Management, Division of Fish and Wildlife. Federal Aid to Fisheries Project, F-20-R-33. Division of Fish & Wildlife. 2p.

Lapin, W.J. and A.D. Libby. 1987. Water Chemistry and Fisheries Investigations of Selected Block Island Ponds. Rhode Island Department of Environmental Management, Division of Fish and Wildlife. Federal Aid in Sport Fish Restoration Act, F-20-R-22, Research Reference Document 87/8. 11p.

Lee, D.S., C.R. Gilbert, C.H. Hocutt, R.E. Jenkins, D.E. McAllister, and J.R. Stauffer, Jr. 1980. Atlas of North American freshwater fishes. Publication #1980-12 of the North Carolina Biological Survey. 854pp.

Libby, A.D. 2007. Stream & Pond Survey. Performance Report. Rhode Island Department of Environmental Management, Division of Fish and Wildlife. Federal Aid to Fisheries Project, F-20-R-48. Division of Fish & Wildlife. 83p. Appendix.

Lyons, J. 1992. The length of stream to sample with a towed electrofishing unit when fish species richness is estimated. North American Journal of Fisheries Management 12:198-203.

McClane, A.J. 1974. Saltwater Fishes of North America. Holt, Rinehart and Winston, NY. 283pp.

Nelson, J.S., E.J. Crossman, H. Espinosa-Perez, L.T. Findley, C.R. Gilbert, R.N. Lea, and J.D. Williams. 2004. Common and scientific names of fishes from the United States, Canada, and Mexico. American Fisheries Society, Special Publication 29, Bethesda, Maryland.

OCI (Office of Compliance and Inspection). 2004. State of Rhode Island 2004 Annual Report to the Governor on the Activities of the dam Safety Program. 27pp.

Page, L.M. and B.M. Burr. 1991. Freshwater Fishes. Houghton Mifflin Company, Boston. 432pp.

Perlmutter, A. 1961. Guide to Marine Fishes. New York University Press. 431pp.

Powell, J.C. 2001. Finfish species of Narragansett Bay and Rhode Island waters. Pages 14-33. in P.V. August, R.W. Enser, and L.L. Gould, editors. Vertebrates of Rhode Island, Volume 2. The Biota of Rhode Island. Rhode Island Natural History Survey.

Raymo, C. and M.E. Raymo. 1989. Written in Stone: A geological and natural history of the Northeaster United States. The Globe Pequot Press, Chester, Connecticut. 163pp.

Robins, C.R and G.C. Ray. 1986. A Field Guide to Atlantic Coast Fishes of North America. Houghton Mifflin Company, Boston. 354pp.

Saila, S.B. and D. Horton. 1957. Fisheries investigations and management in Rhode Island lakes and ponds. Rhode Island Division of Fish and Wildlife Fisheries Publication No. 3. Federal Aid to Fisheries Project, F-2-R. 134pp.

Satchwill, R.J. 2003. The Fisheries Resources of Rhode Island's Coastal Ponds, Tidal Rivers, and Embayments Completion Report. Rhode Island Department of Environmental Management, Division of Fish and Wildlife Federal Aid to Fisheries Project, F-51-R, Rhode Island.

Scarola, J.F. 1973. Freshwater fishes of New Hampshire. New Hampshire Fish and Game Department. 132 pp.

Schmidt, R.E. 1986. Zoogeography of the Northern Appalachians. Pages 137-159. in C.H. Hocutt and E.O. Wiley, editors. The zoogeography of North American freshwater fishes. John Wiley & Sons.

Scott, W.B. and E.J. Crossman. 1973. Freshwater Fishes of Canada. Bulletin 184 of Fisheries Research Board of Canada, Ottawa. 966pp.

Smith, C.L. 1985. The inland fishes of New York state. New York State Department of Environmental Conservation. 522pp.

Steiner, L. 2000. Pennsylvania Fishes. Pennsylvania Fish and Boat Commission. 169pp.

Thomson, E.S., W.H. Weed III, and A.G. Taruski. 1971. Saltwater fishes of Connecticut. Bulletin 105, State Geological and Natural History Survey of Connecticut. 165pp.

Tracy, H.C. 1906. A list of fishes of Rhode Island. *in* Commissioners of Inland Fisheries. 36th Annual Report made to the General Assembly at its January Session, 1906. E.L. Freeman & Sons, Providence, R.I.

Tracy, H.C. 1910. Annotated list of fishes known to inhabit the waters of Rhode Island. *in* Commissioners of Inland Fisheries. Fortieth Annual Report made to the General Assembly at its January Session, 1910. E.L. Freeman & Sons, Providence, R.I.

Wang, J.C.S. and R.J. Kernehan. 1979. Fishes of the Delaware Estuaries. EA Communications, Ecological Analysts, Inc., Towson, Maryland. 410pp.

Werner, R.G. 2004. Freshwater fishes of the Northeastern United States. Syracuse University Press. 335pp.

Whittier, T.R., D.B. Halliwell, and S.G. Paulsen. 1997. Cyprinid distributions in Northeast U.S.A. lakes: evidence of regional-scale minnow biodiversity losses. Canadian Journal of Fisheries and Aquatic Sciences 54:1593-1607.

Whitworth, W.R. 1996. Freshwater Fishes of Connecticut. Second Edition, Bulletin 114, State Geological and Natural History Survey of Connecticut and Department of Environmental Protection. 243pp.

Whitworth, W.R., P.L. Berrien, and W.T. Keller. 1968. Freshwater Fishes of Connecticut. Bulletin 101, State Geological and Natural History Survey of Connecticut, A Division of the Department of Agriculture and Natural Resources. 134pp.

Winston, M.R. and C.M. Taylor. 1991. Upstream Extirpation of Four Minnow Species due to Damming of a Prairie Stream. Transactions of the American Fisheries Society 120:98-105.

Taxonomic Index

Page numbers in **bold** type refer to color plates.
Page numbers in regular type apply to references within the text.